Department of Health
Home Office
Department for Education and Employment

Working Together to Safeguard Children

London

The Stationery Office

Internet Access

The full text of this publication has also been made available to you on the internet.
You can find this at:
https://www.the-stationery-office.co.uk/doh/worktog/worktog.htm
This website also contains links to related publications referenced in the text.
We hope that you will find this feature useful.

The data is held on a secure site that is password protected.
The following information will be required to access the site:

USER NAME: worktog
PASSWORD: safeguard

Please note that both fields are case sensitive and contain no spaces.

ISBN 011 322309 9

Published by The Stationery Office Ltd

Applications for reproduction should be made in writing to:
The Copyright Unit
Her Majesty's Stationery Office
St Clements House
2 – 16 Colegate
Norwich NR3 1BQ

Printed in the United Kingdom for The Stationery Office
J 101107 c1200 12/99

Contents

Preface

The Scope and Purpose of this Document

This document sets out how all agencies and professionals should work together to promote children's welfare and protect them from abuse and neglect. It is addressed to those who work in the health and education services, the police, social services, the probation service, and others whose work brings them into contact with children and families. It is relevant to those working in the statutory, voluntary and independent sectors.

The document:

- describes how actions to safeguard children fit within the wider context of support to children and families;
- summarises some of the lessons learned from research and experience to date on the nature and impact of abuse and neglect, and how best to operate child protection processes;
- sets out the role and responsibilities of different agencies and practitioners;
- outlines the way in which joint working arrangements should be agreed, implemented and reviewed through the mechanism of Area Child Protection Committees;
- sets out the processes which should be followed when there are concerns about a child, and the action which should be taken to safeguard and promote the welfare of children who are suffering, or at risk of suffering, significant harm;
- provides guidance on child protection in specific circumstances, including children living away from home;
- outlines some important principles which should be followed in work with children and families;
- sets out the processes which should be followed if a tragedy occurs, in order to learn lessons and make any necessary improvements in practice to safeguard children; and
- discusses the importance of multi-agency training, and considers training requirements for effective child protection.

The Role of Guidance

This document is intended to provide a national framework within which agencies and professionals at local level - individually and jointly - draw up and agree upon their own more detailed ways of working together.

Processes and procedures are never ends in themselves, but should always be used as a means of bringing about better outcomes for children. No guidance can, or should attempt to, offer a detailed prescription for working with each child and family. Work with children and families where there are concerns about a child's welfare is sensitive and difficult. Good practice calls for effective co-operation between different agencies and professionals; sensitive work with parents and carers in the best interest of the child; and the careful exercise of professional judgement, based on thorough assessment and critical analysis of the available information. To help with the process of assessment, this guidance is complemented by the document, the *Framework for the Assessment of Children in Need and their Families.*

The Status and Content of this Guidance

This guidance is prepared and issued jointly by the Department of Health, the Home Office and the Department for Education. It replaces the previous version of Working Together Under the Children Act 1989, which was published in 1991.

It reflects the principles contained within the United Nations Convention on the Rights of the Child, ratified by the UK Government in 1991. It also takes account the European Convention of Human Rights, in particular Articles 6 and 8. It further takes account of other relevant legislation at the time of publication, but is particularly informed by the requirements of the Children Act 1989, which provides a comprehensive framework for the care and protection of children.

The Children Act 1989 places two specific duties on agencies to co-operate in the interests of vulnerable children:

Section 27 provides that a local authority may request help from:

* any local authority;
* any local education authority;
* any local housing authority;
* any health authority, Special Health Authority or National Health Service Trust; *and*
* any person authorised by the Secretary of State

    in exercising the local authority's functions under Part III of the Act. This part of the Act places a duty on local authorities to provide support and services for children in need, including children looked after by the local authority and those in secure accommodation. The authority whose help is requested in these circumstances has a duty to comply with the request, provided it is compatible with its other duties and functions.

Section 47 places a duty on:

* any local authority;
* any local education authority;
* any housing authority;
* any health authority, Special Health Authority or National Health Service Trust; *and*
* any person authorised by the Secretary of State

to help a local authority with its enquiries in cases where there is reasonable cause to suspect that a child is suffering, or is likely to suffer, significant harm.

This document is issued under Section 7 of the Local Authority Social Services Act 1970, which requires local authorities in their social services functions to act under the general guidance of the Secretary of State. As such, this document does not have the full force of statute, but should be complied with unless local circumstances indicate exceptional reasons which justify a variation.

1

Working together to support children and families

Supporting Children and Families

1.1 All children deserve the opportunity to achieve their full potential. They should be enabled to:

- be as physically and mentally healthy as possible;
- gain the maximum benefit possible from good-quality educational opportunities;
- live in a safe environment and be protected from harm;
- experience emotional well-being;
- feel loved and valued, and be supported by a network of reliable and affectionate relationships;
- become competent in looking after themselves and coping with everyday living;
- have a positive image of themselves, and a secure sense of identity including cultural and racial identity;
- develop good inter-personal skills and confidence in social situations.

If they are denied the opportunity to achieve their potential in this way, children are at risk not only of an impoverished childhood, but they are also more likely to experience disadvantage and social exclusion in adulthood.

1.2 Patterns of family life vary and there is no one, perfect way to bring up children. Good parenting involves caring for children's basic needs, showing them warmth and love and providing the stimulation needed for their development, within a stable environment where they experience consistent guidance and boundaries.

1.3 All parents – supported by friends and family, the wider community and statutory and voluntary services – need to be able to ensure that their children grow up adequately cared for and safe from harm and to promote their children's health and development and help them achieve their potential.

1.4 Parenting can be challenging. It often means juggling with competing priorities to balance work and home life as well as trying to understand how best to meet children's needs at all stages of their development. Parents themselves require and deserve support. Asking for help should be seen as a sign of responsibility rather than as a parenting failure.

1.5 A wide range of services and professionals provide support to families in bringing up children. Both statutory and voluntary services can support families: by helping all children develop to their full potential – for example, through universal education and health services; by providing specialist help to those who need it; and by providing support, or otherwise intervening, at times of adversity or crisis. In the great majority of cases, it should be the decision of parents when to ask for help and advice on their children's care and upbringing. Only in exceptional cases should there be compulsory intervention in family life: for example, where this is necessary to safeguard a child from significant harm. Such intervention should – provided this is consistent with the safety and welfare of the child – support families in making their own plans for the welfare and protection of their children.

1.6 Some children have particular needs, because they are disabled, or because they need certain services in order to achieve or maintain a reasonable standard of health or development, or to prevent their development being impaired. These children are described in the Children Act 1989 as being 'children in need'. They, and possibly also their families may need, or benefit from, a range of extra support and services.

1.7 Some children may be suffering, or at risk of suffering, significant harm, either as a result of a deliberate act, or of a failure on the part of a parent or carer to act or to provide proper care, or both. These children need to be made safe from harm, alongside meeting their other needs.

An Integrated Approach

1.8 Children have varying needs which change over time. Judgements on how best to intervene when there are concerns about harm to a child will often and unavoidably entail an element of risk – at the extreme, of leaving a child for too long in a dangerous situation or of removing a child unnecessarily from their family. The way to proceed in the face of uncertainty is through competent professional judgements based on a sound assessment of the child's needs, the parents' capacity to respond to those needs – including their capacity to keep the child safe from significant harm – and the wider family circumstances.

1.9 Effective measures to safeguard children should not be seen in isolation from the wider range of support and services available to meet the needs of children and families:

- many of the families who become the subject of child protection concerns suffer from multiple disadvantages. Providing services and support to children and families under stress may strengthen the capacity of parents to respond to the needs of their children before problems develop into abuse;

- child protection enquiries may reveal significant unmet needs for support and services among children and families. These should always be explicitly considered, even where concerns are not substantiated about significant harm to a child if the family so wishes;

- if child protection processes are to result in improved outcomes for children, then effective plans for safeguarding children and promoting their welfare should be based on a wide ranging assessment of the needs of the child and their family circum-stances;

- all work with children and families should retain a clear focus on the welfare of the child. Just as child protection processes should always consider the wider needs of the child and family, so broad-based family support services should always be alert to, and know how to respond quickly and decisively to potential indicators of abuse and neglect.

A Shared Responsibility

1.10 Promoting children's well-being and safeguarding them from significant harm depends crucially upon effective information sharing, collaboration and understanding between agencies and professionals. Constructive relationships between individual workers need to be supported by a strong lead from elected or appointed authority members, and the commitment of chief officers.

1.11   At the strategic level, agencies and professionals need to work in partnership with each other and with service users, to plan comprehensive and co-ordinated children's services.

1.12   Individual children, especially some of the most vulnerable children and those at greatest risk of social exclusion, will need co-ordinated help from health, education, social services, and quite possibly the voluntary sector and other agencies, including youth justice services.

1.13   For those children who are suffering, or at risk of suffering significant harm, joint working is essential, to safeguard the child/ren and – where necessary – to help bring to justice the perpetrators of crimes against children. All agencies and professionals should:

- be alert to potential indicators of abuse or neglect;
- be alert to the risks which individual abusers, or potential abusers, may pose to children;
- share and help to analyse information so that an informed assessment can be made of the child's needs and circumstances;
- contribute to whatever actions are needed to safeguard the child and promote his or her welfare;
- regularly review the outcomes for the child against specific shared objectives; *and*
- work co-operatively with parents unless this is inconsistent with the need to ensure the child's safety.

2

Some lessons from research and experience

Introduction

2.1 Our knowledge and understanding of children's welfare – and how to respond in the best interests of a child to concerns about abuse and neglect – develop over time, informed by research, experience and the critical scrutiny of practice. Sound professional practice involves making judgements supported by evidence: evidence derived from research and experience about the nature and impact of abuse and neglect, and when and how to intervene to improve outcomes for children; and evidence derived from thorough assessment about a specific child's health, development and well-being, and his or her family circumstances.

2.2 This chapter begins by setting out what is meant by abuse and neglect; considers their potential impact on a child; and discusses the concept of significant harm. It goes on to summarise some of the messages from research and experience which have informed this guidance, and draws out some messages that have important and enduring implications for policy and practice[1].

Abuse and Neglect

2.3 Somebody may abuse or neglect a child by inflicting harm, or by failing to act to prevent harm. Children may be abused in a family or in an institutional or community setting; by those known to them or, more rarely, by a stranger.

Physical abuse

2.4 Physical abuse may involve hitting, shaking, throwing, poisoning, burning or scalding, drowning, suffocating, or otherwise causing physical harm to a child. Physical harm may also be caused when a parent or carer feigns the symptoms of, or deliberately causes ill health to a child whom they are looking after. This situation is commonly described using terms such as factitious illness by proxy or Munchausen syndrome by proxy.

Emotional Abuse

2.5 Emotional abuse is the persistent emotional ill-treatment of a child such as to cause

---

1. *Acknowledgements*

This chapter draws substantially on the following publications:

Department of Health. *Child Protection: Messages From Research*. London: HMSO, 1995.

Cleaver H, Unell I, Aldgate J. *Children's Needs – Parenting Capacity: The impact of parental mental illness, problem alcohol and drug use, and domestic violence on children's development*. London: The Stationery Office, 1999.

Adcock M, White R (eds.) *Significant Harm: Its Management and Outcome*. Croydon: Significant Publications, 1998.

severe and persistent adverse effects on the child's emotional development. It may involve conveying to children that they are worthless or unloved, inadequate, or valued only insofar as they meet the needs of another person. It may feature age or developmentally inappropriate expectations being imposed on children. It may involve causing children frequently to feel frightened or in danger, or the exploitation or corruption of children. Some level of emotional abuse is involved in all types of ill-treatment of a child, though it may occur alone.

Sexual Abuse

2.6   Sexual abuse involves forcing or enticing a child or young person to take part in sexual activities, whether or not the child is aware of what is happening. The activities may involve physical contact, including penetrative (e.g. rape or buggery) or non-penetrative acts. They may include non-contact activities, such as involving children in looking at, or in the production of, pornographic material or watching sexual activities, or encouraging children to behave in sexually inappropriate ways.

Neglect

2.7   Neglect is the persistent failure to meet a child's basic physical and/or psychological needs, likely to result in the serious impairment of the child's health or development. It may involve a parent or carer failing to provide adequate food, shelter and clothing, failing to protect a child from physical harm or danger, or the failure to ensure access to appropriate medical care or treatment. It may also include neglect of, or unresponsiveness to, a child's basic emotional needs.

The Impact of Abuse and Neglect

2.8   The sustained abuse or neglect of children physically, emotionally or sexually can have major long-term effects on all aspects of a child's health, development and well-being. Sustained abuse is likely to have a deep impact on the child's self-image and self-esteem, and on his or her future life. Difficulties may extend into adulthood: the experience of long-term abuse may lead to difficulties in forming or sustaining close relationships, establishing oneself in the workforce, and to extra difficulties in developing the attitudes and skills needed to be an effective parent.

2.9   It is not only the stressful events of abuse that have an impact, but also the context in which they take place. Any potentially abusive incident has to be seen in context to assess the extent of harm to a child and appropriate intervention. Often, it is the interaction between a number of factors which serve to increase the likelihood or level of actual significant harm.

2.10   For every child and family, there may be factors that aggravate the harm caused to the child, and those that protect against harm. Relevant factors include the individual child's means of coping and adapting, support from a family and social network, and the impact of any interventions. The effects on a child are also influenced by the quality of the family environment at the time of abuse, and subsequent life events. An important point, sometimes overlooked, is that the way in which professionals respond has a significant bearing on subsequent outcomes.

Physical Abuse

2.11   Physical abuse can lead directly to neurological damage, physical injuries, disability or – at the extreme – death. Harm may be caused to children both by the abuse itself, and by the abuse taking place in a wider family or institutional context of conflict and aggression. Physical abuse has been linked to aggressive behaviour in children, emotional and behavioural problems, and educational difficulties.

Emotional Abuse

2.12 There is increasing evidence of the adverse long-term consequences for children's development where they have been subject to sustained emotional abuse. Emotional abuse has an important impact on a developing child's mental health, behaviour and self-esteem. It can be especially damaging in infancy. Underlying emotional abuse may be as important, if not more so, than other more visible forms of abuse in terms of its impact on the child. Domestic violence, adult mental health problems and parental substance misuse may be features in families where children are exposed to such abuse.

Sexual Abuse

2.13 Disturbed behaviour including self-harm, inappropriate sexualised behaviour, sadness, depression and a loss of self-esteem, have all been linked to sexual abuse. Its adverse effects may endure into adulthood. The severity of impact on a child is believed to increase the longer abuse continues, the more extensive the abuse, and the older the child. A number of features of sexual abuse have also been linked with severity of impact, including the extent of premeditation, the degree of threat and coercion, sadism, and bizarre or unusual elements. A child's ability to cope with the experience of sexual abuse, once recognised or disclosed, is strengthened by the support of a non-abusive adult carer who believes the child, helps the child understand the abuse, and is able to offer help and protection.

2.14 A ⸱⸱⸱ of adults who sexually abuse children have themselves been sexually ⸱⸱⸱ also have been exposed as children to domestic violence an⸱ ⸱⸱⸱ vever, it would be quite wrong to suggest that most children who ⸱⸱⸱ ⸱vitably go on to become abusers themselves.

Neglect

2.15 Severe neglect of young children is associated with major impairment of growth and intellectual development. Persistent neglect can lead to serious impairment of health and development, and long term difficulties with social functioning, relationships and educational progress. Neglect can also result, in extreme cases, in death.

The Concept of Significant Harm

2.16 The Children Act 1989 introduced the concept of significant harm as the threshold that justifies compulsory intervention in family life in the best interests of children. The local authority is under a duty to make enquiries, or cause enquiries to be made, where it has reasonable cause to suspect that a child is suffering, or likely to suffer significant harm (s.47). A court may only make a care order (committing the child to the care of the local authority) or supervision order (putting the child under the supervision of a social worker, or a probation officer) in respect of a child if it is satisfied that:

- the child is suffering, or is likely to suffer, significant harm; *and*
- that the harm or likelihood of harm is attributable to a lack of adequate parental care or control (s.31).

2.17 There are no absolute criteria on which to rely when judging what constitutes significant harm. Consideration of the severity of ill-treatment may include the degree and the extent of physical harm, the duration and frequency of abuse and neglect, and the extent of premeditation, degree of threat and coercion, sadism, and bizarre or

> **Under s.31(9) of the Children Act 1989:**
>
> 'harm' means ill-treatment or the impairment of health or development;
>
> 'development' means physical, intellectual, emotional, social or behavioural development;
>
> 'health' means physical or mental health; and
>
> 'ill-treatment' includes sexual abuse and forms of ill-treatment which are not physical.
>
> **Under s.31(10) of the Act:**
>
> Where the question of whether harm suffered by a child is significant turns on the child's health and development, his health or development shall be compared with that which could reasonably be expected of a similar child.

unusual elements in child sexual abuse. Each of these elements has been associated with more severe effects on the child, and/or relatively greater difficulty in helping the child overcome the adverse impact of the ill-treatment. Sometimes, a single traumatic event may constitute significant harm, e.g. a violent assault, suffocation or poisoning. More often, significant harm is a compilation of significant events, both acute and long-standing, which interrupt, change or damage the child's physical and psychological development. Some children live in family and social circumstances where their health and development are neglected. For them, it is the corrosiveness of long-term emotional, physical or sexual abuse that causes impairment to the extent of constituting significant harm. In each case, it is necessary to consider any ill-treatment alongside the family's strengths and supports.

2.18 To understand and establish significant harm, it is necessary to consider:

- the family context;
- the child's development within the context of their family and wider social and cultural environment;
- any special needs, such as a medical condition, communication difficulty or disability that may affect the child's development and care within the family;
- the nature of harm, in terms of ill-treatment or failure to provide adequate care;
- the impact on the child's health and development; *and*
- the adequacy of parental care.

It is important always to take account of the child's reactions, and his or her perceptions, according to the child's age and understanding.

Sources of Stress for Children and Families

2.19 Many families under great stress nonetheless manage to bring up their children in a warm, loving and supportive environment in which the children's needs are met and they are safe from harm. Sources of stress within families may, however, have a negative impact on a child's health, development and well-being, either directly, or because they affect the capacity of parents to respond to their child's needs. This is particularly the case when there is no other significant adult who is able to respond to the child's needs. Research tells us that such sources of stress may include the following.

Social Exclusion

2.20   Many of the families who seek help for their children, or about whom others raise concerns about a child's welfare, are multiply disadvantaged. Many lack a wage earner. Poverty may mean that children live in crowded or unsuitable accommodation, have poor diets, health problems or disability, be vulnerable to accidents, and lack ready access to good educational and leisure opportunities. Racism and racial harassment is an additional source of stress for some families and children.

Domestic Violence

2.21   Prolonged and/or regular exposure to domestic violence can have a serious impact on a child's development and emotional well-being, despite the best efforts of the victim parent to protect the child. Domestic violence has an impact in a number of ways. It can pose a threat to an unborn child, because assaults on pregnant women frequently involve punches or kicks directed at the abdomen, risking injury to both mother and foetus. Older children may also suffer blows during episodes of violence. Children may be greatly distressed by witnessing the physical and emotional suffering of a parent. Both the physical assaults and psychological abuse suffered by adult victims who experience domestic violence can have a negative impact on their ability to look after their children. The negative impact of domestic violence is exacerbated when the violence is combined with drink or drug misuse; children witness the violence; children are drawn into the violence or are pressurised into concealing the assaults. Children's exposure to parental conflict, even where violence is not present, can lead to serious anxiety and distress among children, particularly when it is routed through children.

The Mental Illness of a Parent or Carer

2.22   Mental illness in a parent or carer does not necessarily have an adverse impact on a child, but it is essential always to assess its implications for any children involved in the family. Parental illness may markedly restrict children's social and recreational activities. With both mental and physical illness in a parent, children may have caring responsibilities placed upon them inappropriate to their years, leading them to be worried and anxious. If they are depressed, parents may neglect their own and their children's physical and emotional needs. In some circumstances, some forms of mental illness may blunt parents' emotions and feelings, or cause them to behave towards their children in bizarre or violent ways. Unusually, but at the extreme, a child may be at risk of severe injury, profound neglect, or even death. A study of 100 reviews of child deaths where abuse and neglect had been a factor in the death, showed clear evidence of parental mental illness in one-third of cases. In addition, postnatal depression can also be linked to both behavioural and physiological problems in the infants of such mothers.

2.23   The adverse effects on children of parental mental illness are less likely when parental problems are mild, last only a short time, are not associated with family disharmony, and do not result in the family breaking up. Children may also be protected when the other parent or a family member can help respond to the child's needs. Children most at risk of significant harm are those who feature within parental delusions, and children who become targets for parental aggression or rejection, or who are neglected as a result of parental mental illness.

Drug and Alcohol Misuse

2.24   As with mental illness in a parent, it is important not to generalise, or make assumptions about the impact on a child of parental drug and alcohol misuse. It is, however, important that the implications for the child are properly assessed. Maternal substance misuse in pregnancy may impair the development of an unborn child. A parent's practical caring skills may be diminished by misuse of drugs and/or alcohol. Some substance misuse may give rise to mental states or behaviour that put children at risk of injury, psychological distress or neglect. Children are particularly vulnerable when parents are withdrawing from drugs. The risk will be greater when the adult's substance misuse is chaotic or otherwise out of control. Some substance misusing parents may find it difficult to give priority to the needs of their children, and finding money for drugs and/or alcohol may reduce the money available to the household to meet basic needs, or may draw families into criminal activities. Children may be at risk of physical harm if drugs and paraphernalia (e.g. needles) are not kept safely out of reach. Some children have been killed through inadvertent access to drugs (e.g. methadone stored in a fridge). In addition, children may be in danger if they are a passenger in a car whilst a drug/ alcohol misusing carer is driving.

Child Protection Processes

2.25 In 1995, the Department of Health published *Child Protection: Messages from Research*, which summarised the key findings from 20 research studies commissioned by the Department through its child protection research programme. A number of important themes emerged about the operation of child protection processes during the period covered by the research:

* some professionals were using s.47 enquiries inappropriately, as a means of obtaining services for children in need;

* over half of the children and families who were the subject of s.47 enquiries received no services as the result of professionals' interest in their lives. Too often, enquiries were too narrowly conducted as investigations into whether abuse or neglect had occurred, without considering the wider needs and circumstances of the child and family;

* enquiries into suspicions of child abuse can have traumatic effects on families. Good professional practice can ease parents' anxiety and lead to co-operation that helps to safeguard the child. As nearly all children remain at, or return home, involving the family in child protection processes is likely to be effective. Professionals could still do more to work in partnership with parents and the child;

* discussions at child protection conferences tended to focus too heavily on decisions about registration and removal, rather than focusing on future plans to safeguard the child and support the family in the months after the conference;

* while inter-agency work was often relatively good at the early stages of enquiries, its effectiveness tended to decline once child protection plans had been made, with social services left with sole responsibility for implementing the plans;

* there was inconsistent use made of the child protection register, which was not consulted for 60% of children for whom there were child protection concerns.

Some Implications for Policy and Practice

2.26 The research summarised in this chapter gives rise to some important lessons for policy and practice, among them:

Focus on Outcomes for the Child

* consider what interventions are intended to achieve, and what will be the benefits to the child's long-term well-being;

* invest sufficient time and resources across all relevant agencies in planning and

implementing interventions to safeguard and promote the welfare of children at continuing risk of significant harm. Aim for good long-term outcomes in terms of health, development and educational achievement for children about whom there are child protection concerns;

Child Protection in Context

- promote access to a range of services for children in need without inappropriately triggering child protection processes;
- consider the wider needs of children and families involved in child protection processes, whether or not concerns about abuse and/or neglect are substantiated;

Work with Children and Families

- listen to children and take their views into account;
- enable parents and other family members to be as fully involved as practicable, ensuring the child's safety and welfare;
- negative initial experiences influence parents' future relationships with the professionals. Set a constructive tone for future intervention through the quality of work when concerns are first raised about a child's welfare;
- many families fear that revealing their problems will lead to punitive reactions by service providers. Promote a positive but realistic image of services to encourage and enable people to gain access to the help and advice they need. Families need information on how to gain access to services and what to expect if and when they approach services for help;

Skilled Assessment

- look at the whole picture – not only what has happened to the child, but also the child's health and development, and the wider family and environmental context;
- be aware of the many factors that may affect a parent's ability to care for a child, and that these can have an impact on children in many different ways;
- build on families' strengths, while addressing difficulties;
- make full use of existing sources of information, including the Child Protection Register;

Working across Adult and Children's Services

- while recognising that the child's safety and welfare are paramount, give due consideration to the needs of all family members;
- recognise the complementary roles of adult and children's services in health and social care. For example, understanding the implications for a patient suffering from severe depression who is also a parent should be the responsibility of both adult mental health staff and children and families staff. Pool expertise to strengthen parents' capacity to respond to their children's needs, where this is in the best interests of the child;
- professionals who work primarily with children may need training to recognise and identify parents' problems and the effects these may have on children. Equally, training for professionals working with adults should cover the impact parental problems may have on children. Joint training between adult and children's staff can be useful;

* even among staff who work with children, there can be gaps (in particular between children and families staff and those working in specialist teams for disabled children) which need to be bridged.

The Framework for the Assessment of Children in Need and their Families

2.27 The *Framework for the Assessment of Children in Need and their Families* provides the foundation for a systematic assessment of children and families, and is referred to at several points in this guidance. The framework embraces three key areas: the child's developmental needs; parental capacity; and wider family and environmental factors. The process draws on the contribution of a range of agencies in contributing to assessments and providing services. The framework makes clear that assessment is a process, not a single event, and that action and services should be provided in parallel with assessment according to the needs of the child and family. A short summary of the framework is at Appendix 1.

3

Roles and responsibilities

Introduction

3.1 An awareness and appreciation of the role of others is essential for effective collaboration. This section outlines the main roles and responsibilities of statutory agencies, professionals, the voluntary sector, and the wider community, in relation to child protection. Joint working should extend across the planning, management, provision and delivery of services.

Local Authorities

3.2 The welfare of children is a corporate responsibility of the entire local authority, working in partnership with other public agencies, the voluntary sector, and service users and carers. All local authority services have an impact on the lives of children and families, and local authorities have a particular responsibility towards those children and families most at risk of social exclusion. Local authorities have a duty to plan services for children in need, in consultation with a wide range of other agencies, and to publish the resulting children's services plans. The local authority should also take the lead responsibility for the establishment and effective functioning of Area Child Protection Committees (ACPCs) – the inter-agency forum which acts as a focal point for local co-operation to safeguard children.

3.3 In thinking more corporately about what will benefit local citizens, some authorities have put in place management structures which cut across traditional departmental and service boundaries. Some authorities, for example, have put in place management arrangements which bring together a range of services affecting children. Where this guidance refers to social services departments, it means that part of the local authority which carries out social services' functions.

Social Services

3.4 A key objective for social services departments is to ensure that children are protected from significant harm. They provide a wide range of care and support for adults, children and families, including: older people; people with physical or learning disabilities; people with mental health or substance misuse problems; ex-offenders and young offenders; families, especially where children have special needs; children at risk of harm; children who need to be accommodated or looked after by the local authority, through fostering or residential care, and children who are placed for adoption.

3.5 Social services' responsibilities towards children should be seen in the context of this broad range of social care and support, so that children and families can be helped and supported in an integrated way which recognises the range and diversity of their needs and strengths.

3.6 Local authorities, acting in order to fulfill their social services functions, have specific legal duties in respect of children under the Children Act 1989. They have a general duty to safeguard and promote the welfare of children in their area who are in need, and – provided that this is consistent with the child's safety and welfare – to promote the upbringing of such children by their families, by providing services appropriate to the child's needs (s.17). They should do this in partnership with parents and in a way which is sensitive to the child's race, religion, culture and language. Services might include day care for young children, after school care for school children, counselling, respite care, family centres or practical help in the home. Social services are rarely the only agency in contact with vulnerable children and their families, and partnerships with other agencies – especially health and education – are essential to help support such children and families.

3.7 Social services departments also have a duty to make enquiries if they have reason to suspect that a child in their area is suffering, or likely to suffer significant harm, to enable them to decide whether they should take any action to safeguard or promote the child's welfare (s.47). They need the help of other agencies in order to do this effectively. When approaching other agencies with requests for information, it is important that social services staff are clear about the nature and purpose of the request. In particular, clarity is needed about whether the consent of the subject of the information requested has been obtained or whether, in the view of social services, such consent-seeking would itself place a child at risk of significant harm. This will enable those who receive such requests to judge whether the duty to maintain confidentiality should be breached in the circumstances of the particular case.

3.8 A child who is at risk of significant harm will invariably be a child in need. The social services department is responsible for co-ordinating an assessment of the child's needs, the parents' capacity to keep the child safe and promote his or her welfare, and of the wider family circumstances. In the great majority of cases, children are safeguarded from harm by working with parents, family members and other significant adults in the child's life to make the child safe, and to promote his or her development, within the family setting. Where a child is at continuing risk of significant harm, social services are responsible for co-ordinating a inter-agency plan to safeguard the child, which sets out and draws upon the contributions of family members, professionals and other agencies. In a few cases, the social services department, in consultation with other involved agencies and professionals, may judge that a child's welfare can not be sufficiently safeguarded if he or she remains at home. In these circumstances, the social services department may apply to the courts for a Care Order, which commits the child to the care of the local authority. Where the child is thought to be in immediate danger, the social services department may apply to the courts for an Emergency Protection Order, which places the child under the protection of the local authority for a maximum of eight days.

3.9 Because of their responsibilities, duties and powers in relation to vulnerable children, social services departments act as the principal point of contact for children about whom there are child welfare concerns. They may be contacted directly by parents or family members seeking help, concerned friends and neighbours, or by professionals and others from statutory and voluntary agencies.

Education Services

3.10 All those working in the education services can contribute to the safeguarding of children and child protection processes. All schools and colleges have a pastoral responsibility towards their pupils. They can play a part in the prevention of abuse and neglect, through their own policies and procedures for safeguarding children, and through the curriculum. All schools and colleges should create and maintain a safe environment for children and young people, and should be able to manage situations where there are child welfare concerns. Children can be helped to understand what is and is not acceptable behaviour towards them, and taught about staying safe from harm, and how to speak up if they have worries or concerns. The curriculum can also play a preventive role in developing awareness and resilience and in preparing children and young people for their future responsibilities as adults, parents and citizens.

3.11 Through their day to day contact with pupils, and direct work with families, education staff have a crucial role to play in noticing indicators of possible abuse or neglect, and in referring concerns to the appropriate agency, normally the social services department. When a child has special educational needs, or is disabled, schools will have important information about the child's level of understanding and the most effective means of communicating with the child. They will also be well placed to give a view on the impact of treatment or intervention on the child's care or behaviour.

3.12 Staff working in the education service will on occasions be asked by a social services department for information on a child about whom there are concerns about abuse or neglect. The education service itself does not have a direct investigative responsibility in child protection work, but schools and other maintained establishments have a role in assisting the social services department by referring concerns and providing information for s.47 child protection enquiries.

3.13 Where a child of school age is the subject of an inter-agency child protection plan, the school should be involved in the preparation of the plan. The school's role and responsibilities in contributing to actions to safeguard the child, and promote his or her welfare, should be clearly identified.

3.14 Throughout the education service:
- all staff should be alert to the signs of abuse and neglect, and know to whom they should report concerns or suspicions;
- all schools and colleges should have a designated member of staff with knowledge and skills in recognising and acting upon child protection concerns. He or she should act as a source of expertise and advice, and is responsible for co-ordinating action within the institution and liasing with other agencies;
- all schools and colleges should be aware of the child protection procedures established by the ACPC and, where appropriate, the Local Education Authority (LEA);
- all schools and colleges should have procedures for handling suspected cases of abuse, including procedures to be followed if a member of staff is accused of abuse;
- staff with designated responsibility for child protection should receive appropriate training;
- the school health service has a vital role to play in promoting and maintaining the health of school children and in safeguarding and promoting their welfare;
- school governors should exercise their child protection responsibilities, in particular in response to allegations against headteachers, and in ensuring that there are school child protection policies in place;
- in every LEA a senior officer should be responsible for co-ordinating action on child protection issues across the Authority;
- all schools should have an effective whole school policy against bullying and

headteachers should have measures in place to prevent all forms of bullying among pupils;

* where a state school is concerned that a child may have 'disappeared', or about any aspect of a pupil transfer which gives rise to concerns about a child's welfare, it should report its concerns to a person specified in ACPC guidance, or to the LEA officer with designated responsibility for child protection;

* corporal punishment is outlawed for all pupils in all schools and colleges, including independent schools;

* teachers at a school are allowed to use reasonable force to control or restrain pupils under certain circumstances. Other people may also do so, in the same way as teachers, provided they have been authorised by the head teacher to have control or charge of pupils. All schools should have a policy about the use of force to control or restrain pupils.

Independent Schools

3.15   The role of independent schools in relation to child protection is the same as that of any other school. The same pastoral responsibilities apply, and schools should adopt the principles and pursue the objectives contained within this guidance (see para. 6.5). It is particularly important that independent schools (including independent special schools) establish channels of communication with local social services departments and ACPCs, building on existing links with the local education authority, so that children requiring support receive prompt attention and any allegations of abuse can be properly investigated. Independent schools which provide medical and/or nursing care should ensure that their medical and nursing staff have appropriate training and access to advice on child protection. Social services departments and ACPCs offer the same level of support and advice to independent schools in matters of child protection as they do to maintained schools.

Youth Services

3.16   Youth and Community Workers (YCWs) have close contacts with children and young people, and should be alert to signs of abuse and neglect and know how to act upon concerns about a child's welfare. Local Authority youth services should provide written instructions, consistent with local ACPC procedures, on the circumstances in which YCWs should consult colleagues, line managers, and other statutory authorities when they have concerns about a child or young person. The instructions should emphasise the importance of safeguarding and promoting the welfare of the young people while acknowledging the importance of maintaining confidentiality between the young person and the YCW, insofar as this is consistent with the young person's welfare. Local voluntary youth organisations should seek guidance from their national bodies, or from the ACPC, on how best to safeguard the children and young people for whom they are providing a service.

Cultural and Leisure Services

3.17   Cultural and leisure services provide and enable a wide range of facilities and services for children. By the nature of these activities, leisure staff, volunteers and others contracted by departments are in various degrees of contact with children. Such departments should therefore have in place procedures which are linked with local ACPC procedures, detailing referral and other responses to information that may arise concerning child protection concerns, and the requirements for staff training for those working with children. Working practices and procedures should be adopted that minimise situations where abuse of children may occur, such as unobserved contact. It is also good practice to draw up and disseminate widely codes of practice for coaches, parents and children's participation in activities provided by departments.

Health Services

General

3.18 All health professionals, in the NHS, private sector, and other agencies, play an essential part in ensuring that children and families receive the care, support and services they need in order to promote children's health and development. Because of the universal nature of health provision, health professionals are often the first to be aware that families are experiencing difficulties in looking after their children.

3.19 The involvement of health professionals is important at all stages of work with children and families:

- recognising children in need of support and/or safeguarding, and parents who may need extra help in bringing up their children;
- contributing to enquiries about a child and family;
- assessing the needs of children and the capacity of parents to meet their children's needs;
- planning and providing support to vulnerable children and families;
- participating in child protection conferences;
- planning support for children at risk of significant harm;
- providing therapeutic help to abused children and parents under stress (e.g. mental illness);
- playing a part, through the child protection plan, in safeguarding children from significant harm; *and*
- contributing to case reviews.

There will always be a need for close co-operation with other agencies, including any other health professionals involved.

The Health Authority

3.20 The health authority should take the overall strategic lead for health services in local inter-agency working on child protection matters. It should co-operate with other agencies, especially the local authority, in planning services for vulnerable children and their families, and ensuring that local health agencies and professionals contribute fully and effectively to local inter-agency working to safeguard children and promote their welfare. This responsibility includes ensuring that there is suitable health service involvement in, and commitment to, the work of the ACPC. This involves ensuring the provision of advice and support to the ACPC in respect of a range of specialist health functions e.g. primary care, mental health (adult and child and adolescent) and sexual health. It also includes co-ordinating the health component of case reviews (see Chapter 8). To the extent that they commission health services, health authorities should ensure that service specifications should include clear service standards for safeguarding children and promoting their welfare, consistent with local ACPC procedures.

3.21 Each health authority is responsible for identifying a senior paediatrician, and a senior nurse with a health visiting qualification (designated senior professionals) to take a professional lead on all aspects of the health service contribution to safeguarding children. Designated professionals are a vital source of professional advice on child protection matters to other professionals and to social services departments. They will play an important role in promoting and influencing relevant training, skilled professional involvement in child protection processes in line with ACPC protocols, and participation in case reviews. They should comprise part of the local health service representation on the ACPC. The designated professionals will normally be based in a Trust, but will have responsibilities across the health authority area. In this authority-wide capacity, they should establish regular contact with named professionals in Trusts (including Primary Care Trusts, see para. 3.23). Their roles should always be explicitly defined in their job descriptions and they should be allowed sufficient time to fulfil their child protection responsibilities effectively. Appointment as a designated professional does not, in itself, signify responsibility personally for providing a full clinical service for child protection. This should be the subject of separate agreements with relevant Trusts. In developing such agreements, it is important to ensure that health professionals are provided with access to those who can provide expert advice on child protection matters.

Hospitals and Community Health Services

3.22   NHS Trusts and Primary Care Groups/Trusts (PCG/Ts) are responsible for providing acute and community health services in hospital and community settings, and a wide range of staff will come into contact with children and parents in the course of their normal duties. Staff should be trained to be alert to potential indicators of abuse or neglect in children, and know how to act upon their concerns in line with local ACPC procedures.

3.23   Each NHS Trust – including PGC/Ts – is recommended to identify a named doctor and a named nurse or midwife who will take a professional lead within the Trust on child protection matters. The named doctor and nurse should have expertise in children's health and development, the nature of child maltreatment, and local arrangements for safeguarding children and promoting their welfare. They provide an important source of advice and expertise for fellow professionals and other agencies, and also have an important role in promoting good professional practice within the Trust in safeguarding children. They are responsible for conducting the Trust's internal case reviews (see Chapter 8) except where they have had substantial personal involvement in a case.

3.24   All hospital and community health staff should be alert to the possibility of child abuse or neglect, be aware of local procedures know the names and contact details of the relevant named and designated professionals. Any concerns staff have about a child should be acted on in accordance with Chapter 5 of this document, with advice being sought from named professionals as appropriate. Staff working in Accident and Emergency (A&E) departments and minor injury centres should be familiar with local procedures for making enquiries of the child protection register. They should be alert to carers who seek medical care from a number of sources in order to conceal the repeated nature of a child's injuries. Specialist paediatric advice should be available at all times to A&E Departments, and all wards where children receive care. If a child – or children from the same household – presents repeatedly, even with slight injuries, in a way which doctors, nurses and other staff find worrying, they should act upon their concerns in accordance with Chapter 5 of this guidance. All visits by children to an A&E department should be notified quickly to the child's primary health care team and should be recorded in the child's hospital notes, if there are any. The health visitor and school nurse should also be notified where such professionals have a role in relation to the child.

Primary Care Groups and Primary Care Trusts

3.25   Primary Care Groups (PCGs) are bodies covering groups of GP Practices and are responsible for improving the health of their combined practice population, developing primary and community health services, and commissioning hospital and community health services. Many PGCs are expected to become Primary Care Trusts (PCTs), free-standing statutory bodies responsible for commissioning hospital and community health services, or in some circumstances, providing community health services directly themselves.

3.26   The health authority should, through agreement with PGC/Ts, ensure that the local health service contribution to inter-agency working is discharged.

3.27   Service specifications drawn up by PCG/Ts as commissioners should include clear service standards for safeguarding children and promoting their welfare, consistent with local ACPC procedures.

The General Practitioner and the Primary Health Care Team

3.28   The general practitioner (GP) and other members of the primary health care team (PHCT) are well placed to recognise when a child is potentially in need of extra help or services to promote health and development, or is at risk of harm. Surgery consultations, home visits, treatment room sessions, child health clinic attendance, and information from PHCT staff such as health visitors, midwives and practice nurses may all help to build up a picture of the child's situation and can alert the team if something is amiss. All PHCT members should know when it is appropriate to refer a child to social services for help as a 'child in need', and how to act on concerns that a child may be at risk of significant harm through abuse or neglect. When other members of the PHCT become concerned about the welfare of a child action should be taken in accordance with local procedures. In addition, the GP should be informed straightaway. All PHCT members should know how to contact colleagues who have experience in child protection matters, such as named professionals within their trust or social services, in cases where there is any uncertainty.

3.29   The GP and the PHCT are also well placed to recognise when a parent or other adult has problems which may affect their capacity as a parent or carer, or which may mean that they pose a risk of harm to a child. While GPs have responsibilities to all their patients, the child is particularly vulnerable and the welfare of the child is paramount. If the PHCT has concerns that an adult's problems or behaviour may be causing, or putting a child at risk of significant harm, they should follow the procedures set out in Chapter 5 of this guidance.

3.30   Because of their knowledge of children and families, GPs (together with other PHCT members) have an important role in all stages of child protection processes, from sharing information with social services when enquiries are being made about a child, to involvement in a child protection plan to safeguard a child. GPs should make available to child protection conferences relevant information about a child and family, whether or not they – or a member of the PHCT – are able to attend.

3.31   GPs should take part in child protection training and have regular updates as part of their postgraduate educational programme. As employers, GPs are responsible for their staff and therefore should ensure that practice nurses, practice managers, receptionists and any other staff whom they employ, are given the opportunities to attend local child protection courses, or undergo such training within the practice team, including on a whole PHCT joint basis.

3.32 It is good practice to have a clear means of identifying in records those children (together with their parents and siblings) who are on the child protection register. This will enable them to be recognised by the partners of the practice and any other doctor, practice nurse or health visitor who may be involved in the care of those children. There should be good communication between GPs, health visitors, practice nurses and midwives in respect of all children about whom there are concerns.

3.33 Each GP and member of the PHCT should have access to an up to date copy of the local Area Child Protection Committee's procedures.

The Midwife, Health Visitor and School Nurse

3.34 Nurses work with children and families in a variety of environments and are well placed to recognise when a child is in need of help, services or at potential risk of significant harm.

3.35 The primary focus of health visitors' work with families is health promotion. Like few other professional groups, health visitors provide a universal service which, coupled with their knowledge of children and families and their expertise in assessing and monitoring child health and development, means they have an important role to play in all stages of family support and child protection. Health visitors are often the starting point for child protection referrals and their continuing work in supporting families places them in an unique position to continue to play an important part as enquiries progress.

3.36 Midwives are involved with parents from the confirmation of the pregnancy through until some time after the baby's birth. As well as working with their clients to ensure a healthy pregnancy and offering education on childcare and parenting, the close relationship they foster with their clients provides an opportunity to observe attitudes towards the developing baby and identify potential problems during pregnancy, birth and the child's early care.

3.37 School nurses have regular contact with school age children who spend a significant proportion of their time in school. Their skills and knowledge of child health and development mean that, in their work with children in promoting, assessing and monitoring health and development, they have important role in all stages of child protection processes.

3.38 Nurses, midwives and school nurses must be provided with child protection training and have regular updates as part of their post registration educational programme.

All Mental Health Services

3.39 All professionals working in mental health services in the statutory, voluntary and independent sectors, should bear in mind the welfare of children, irrespective of whether they are primarily working with adults or with children and young people. They are likely to become aware of a broad range of children's needs in their daily work. All mental health professionals should be aware of the legislation concerning child protection and informed about their local child protection procedures and the workings of the ACPC, and of their responsibilities for safeguarding children. They may need to fulfil their duty to assist social services in assessments, as well as by attending and reporting to child protection conferences when necessary.

3.40 The mental health perspective is important in respect of many aspects of children's welfare. ACPCs should be able to call upon the expertise of child and adolescent mental health services, learning disability, adult, forensic and substance misuse services.

3.41 Adult mental health services, including forensic services, together with child and adolescent mental health services, have a role to play in assessing the risk posed by adult perpetrators, and in the provision of treatment services for perpetrators. In particular cases, the expertise of substance misuse and learning disability services will also be required.

Child and Adolescent Mental Health Services

3.42 In the course of their work, child and adolescent mental health professionals will inevitably identify or suspect instances where a child may have been abused and/or neglected. They should follow the child protection procedures laid own for their services within their area. Consultation, supervision and training resources should be available and accessible in each service.

3.43 Child and adolescent mental health professionals may have a role in the initial assessment process in circumstances where their specific skills and knowledge are helpful. Examples include: children and young people with severe behavioural and emotional disturbance, such as eating disorders or self-harming behaviour; families where there is a perceived high risk of danger; very young children, or where the abused child or abuser have severe communication problems; situations where parent or carer feigns the symptoms of or deliberately causes ill-health to a child; and where multiple victims are involved. In addition, assessment and treatment services may need to be provided to young mentally disordered offenders. The assessment of children and adults with significant learning difficulties, a disability, or sensory and communication difficulties, may require the expertise of a psychiatrist in learning disability or a specialist child psychiatrist.

3.44 Child and adolescent mental health services have a role in the provision of a range of psychiatric and psychological assessment and treatment services for children and families. Services that may be provided, in liaison with social services, include the provision of reports for Court, and direct work with children, parents and families. Services may be provided either within general or specialist multidisciplinary teams, depending upon the severity and complexity of the problem. In addition, consultation and training may be offered to services in the community including, for example social services, schools, Primary Health Care Teams, nurseries.

Adult Mental Health Services

3.45 Adult mental health services, including those providing general adult and community, forensic, psychotherapy, alcohol and substance misuse and learning disability services, have a responsibility in safeguarding children when they become aware of or identify a child at risk of harm. This may be as a result of service's direct work with those who may be mentally ill, a parent, a parent-to-be, or a non-related abuser, or in response to a request for the assessment of an adult perceived to represent a potential or actual risk to a child or young person.

3.46 Close collaboration and liaison between the adult mental health services and children's welfare services are essential in the interests of children. This will require the sharing of information where this is necessary to safeguard a child from significant harm. Child and adolescent mental health services can help in facilitating communication between adult mental health services and children's welfare services, especially when there are concerns about responding appropriately both to the duty of confidentiality and the protection of children. The named doctor and/or named nurse can also provide advice.

Visiting of Psychiatric Patients By Children

3.47 There are two specific areas regarding children visiting parents and other family members in psychiatric settings where social services departments may be asked to assess whether it is in the best interests of a child to visit a named patient.

3.48 The Directions and associated guidance to Ashworth, Broadmoor and Rampton Hospital Authorities (HSC 1999/160) sets out the assessment process to be followed when deciding whether a child can visit a named patient in these hospitals. When a social services department considers it has powers under the Children Act 1989 to undertake the necessary assessment, it should assist the hospital by assessing whether it is in the interests of a particular child to visit a named patient (LAC(99)23).

3.49 The Guidance on the Visiting of Psychiatric Patients by Children (HSC 1999/222: LAC (99)32) to NHS Trusts, health authorities and social services departments, on the implementation of the guidance at paragraph 26.3 of the revised Mental Health Act 1983 Code of Practice, published in April 1999 states that:

> "Hospitals should have written policies on the arrangements about the visiting of patients by children, which should be drawn up in consultation with local social services authorities. A visit by a child should only take place following a decision that such a visit would be in the child's best interests. Decisions to allow such visits should be regularly reviewed."

3.50 The guidance also sets out principles to underpin child visiting policies in respect of children visiting patients detained under the Mental Health Act. This emphasises the importance of facilitating a child's contact with their parents or other key family members, wherever possible. Where there are child welfare concerns, the Trust may ask the social services department to assess whether it is in the best interests of a child to visit a named patient.

Drug Services

3.51 A range of services is provided, in particular by health and voluntary organisations, to respond to the needs of both adults (with parental responsibilities) and children who misuse drugs. These services are linked to the relevant agencies at local level through Drug Action Teams which comprise, as a minimum, health, social services, education and police representatives. It is important that arrangements are in place, at ACPC level, which enable child protection and substance misuse referrals to be made in relevant cases. Where children may be suffering significant harm because of their own substance misuse, or where parental misuse may be causing such harm, referrals will need to be made by drug services in accordance with ACPC procedures. Where children are not suffering significant harm, referral arrangements also need to be in place to enable children's broader needs to be assessed and responded to.

Other Health Professionals

3.52 Many other health professionals provide help and support to promote children's health and development, and many work with vulnerable children and families who experience problems in looking after children. The following should be aware of local ACPC procedures:

- accident and emergency staff;
- ambulance service staff;
- clinical psychologists;
- dental practitioners;
- staff in genito-urinary medicine services;
- obstetric and gynaecological staff;
- occupational therapists;

- physiotherapists;
- staff working in private health care;
- staff in sexual health services, pregnancy advisory services;
- speech and language therapists; *and*
- other professions allied to medicine.

They should receive the training and supervision needed to recognise and act upon child welfare concerns, and to respond to the needs of children.

3.53 NHS Direct is a 24-hour telephone line, usually staffed by nurses, giving direct access to health information and advice. Its staff should also have access to clear procedures, training and advice on child protection.

Day Care Services

3.54 Day care services – family centres, early years centres, nurseries (including workplace nurseries), childminders, playgroups and holiday and out of school schemes – play an increasingly important part in the lives of large numbers of children. Many services will be offering help to families and children with problems and stresses. This makes them well placed to help prevent problems from developing into abuse and neglect through support to families, and to recognise and act upon potential indicators of abuse and neglect.

3.55 All those providing day care services should know how to recognise and respond to potential indicators of abuse or neglect, and should know what to do when they have concerns about a child's welfare. Day care providers in the private and voluntary sectors should have agreed procedures for when and how to contact the social services department about an individual child.

3.56 Day care services can play an important part in supporting families under stress, including families where a child is at risk of significant harm. By helping children directly and by supporting parents, day care services can contribute to a child's welfare and to keeping the child safe from harm, and can strengthen the capacity of parents to meet their child's needs. Many day care services have considerable experience of working with families where a child needs to be safeguarded from harm, and many local authorities provide, commission or sponsor specific services, including child-minders, to work with children in need and their families.

The Police

3.57 Protecting life and preventing crime are primary tasks of the police. Children are citizens who have the right to the protection offered by the criminal law. The police have a duty and responsibility to investigate criminal offences committed against children, and such investigations should be carried out sensitively, thoroughly and professionally.

3.58 The police recognise the fundamental importance of inter-agency working in combating child abuse, as illustrated by well-established arrangements for joint training involving police and social work colleagues. The police have invested a great deal in both training and resources, to enhance their ability to offer the best possible service to child victims of crime. All Forces have child protection units (CPUs), and despite variations in their structures and staffing levels, they will normally take primary responsibility for investigating child abuse cases. Ideally, CPU staff should, as a minimum, investigate all aspects of child abuse allegations within the family, or committed by a carer, where the victim is under 18 years of age. It is important therefore that such units include sufficient staff with investigative experience commensurate with the serious nature of their work.

3.59 It is also important that safeguarding children is not, within a policing context, seen as solely the role of CPU officers, but that all police officers understand it is a fundamental part of their duties. Patrol officers attending domestic violence incidents, for example, should be aware of the effect of such violence on any children within the household. Community Beat Officers should be made aware of any children in their area who are on the Child Protection Register, perhaps through links with Police information systems.

3.60 The police are committed to sharing information and intelligence with other agencies where this is necessary to protect children. This includes a responsibility to ensure that those officers representing the Force at a child protection conference are fully informed about the case as well as being experienced in risk assessment and the decision-making process. Similarly, they can expect other agencies to share with them information and intelligence they hold to enable the police to carry out their duties. Evidence gathered during a criminal investigation may be of use to local authority solicitors who are preparing for civil proceedings to protect the victim. The Crown Prosecution Service (CPS) should be consulted, but evidence will normally be shared if it is in the best interests of the child.

3.61 The police should be notified as soon as possible where a criminal offence has been committed, or is suspected of having been committed, against a child. This does not mean that in all such cases a criminal investigation will be required, or that there will necessarily be any further police involvement. It is important, however, that the police retain the opportunity to be informed and consulted, to ensure all relevant information can be taken into account before a final decision is made. Chapter 5 states that ACPCs should have in place a protocol agreed between social services departments and the police, to guide both agencies in deciding how child protection enquiries should be conducted and, in particular, the circumstances in which joint enquiries are appropriate.

3.62 The decision as to whether or not criminal proceedings should be initiated are based on three main factors: whether or not there is sufficient evidence to prosecute; whether it is in the public interest that proceedings should be instigated against a particular offender; and whether or not a criminal prosecution is in the best interests of the child. Although the police may commence proceedings, it is the responsibility of the CPS to review the evidence and, where appropriate, conduct all criminal prosecutions. In some cases, advice from the CPS will be sought prior to proceedings being initiated. In dealing with offences involving a child victim, the police will normally work in partnership with social services and other caring agencies. Whilst the responsibility to instigate criminal proceedings rests with the police, they should always obtain and consider the views expressed by other partners about what is in a child's best interests.

3.63 The evidential standard required by the criminal court is proof 'beyond reasonable doubt' that the defendant committed the offence. The burden of proof rests with the prosecution; defendants do not have to prove their innocence. Proceedings for the protection of children under the Children Act 1989 take place in the civil court which work to a different standard of proof, that of the 'balance of probabilities'. It is not unusual for the police or the CPS to decide that criminal proceedings cannot be instigated against a person suspected of child abuse on the grounds that there is insufficient evidence to meet the higher standard of proof, whilst a civil court is still able to decide that the child needs protection from the same person. The criminal courts focus on the behaviour of the defendant; the civil courts on the interests of the child.

3.64 In addition to their duty to investigate criminal offences the police have emergency powers to enter premises and ensure the immediate protection of children believed to be suffering from, or at risk of, significant harm. Such powers should be used only when necessary, the principle being that wherever possible the decision to remove a child from a parent or carer should be made by a court.

Probation Services

3.65 Probation services have a statutory duty to supervise offenders effectively in order to reduce offending and protect the public. In the execution of that duty probation officers will be in contact with, or supervising, a number of men (and, to a far lesser extent, women) who have convictions for offences against children. Further, probation services will also be working with those who have children who may be in need and those whose convictions relate to domestic violence. Probation services will be supervising dangerous child sex offenders on licence after release from prison and, more generally, will also work with a range of offenders with convictions for less serious offences against children. The risk posed by such offenders may relate to children in the community in general or to specific children with whom offenders are (or are likely to be) living.

3.66 In addition, specialist probation officers working in the Family Courts may be alerted to alleged or actual child abuse through their investigations as Court Welfare Officers. All staff may, in the normal course of their work in the community, become concerned about the safety of a child or children. Probation services work closely with the police, social services departments and other relevant organisations to assess the risk posed to children by known and suspected offenders. Inter-agency case conferences, focusing on the necessary action to manage the risk posed by offenders, have been introduced following the Sex Offender Act 1997, with its requirement for sex offenders to register with the police. Such conferences, often known as risk management meetings or panels, also agree action plans for potentially dangerous offenders who fall outside the remit of the Sex Offender Act 1997. These processes, which in many ways parallel child protection conferences, but with the focus on managing the risk posed by the perpetrator, are central to the inter-agency approach supported by probation services. They operate according to written protocols which have been agreed by the agencies involved.

3.67 In any case where an imprisoned offender is considered to pose a risk to children, the social services department in the area where the offender lives (or intends to live in the case of prisoners) should be alerted and an inter-agency approach adopted. Probation services are required to work closely with social services and the prison service in such cases, and have a central role in the resettlement of such prisoners.

The Prison Service

3.68 The prison service works closely with other agencies to identify any prisoner who may represent a risk to the public on release. Regular risk assessments take account of progress made during the sentence, and inform decisions on sentence planning for individual prisoners, including sex offender treatment programmes. Governors are required to notify social services departments and the probation service of plans to release prisoners convicted of offences against children and young people so that appropriate action can be taken by agencies in the community to minimise any risk.

3.69 The prison service recognises the importance for children of being able to maintain contact with a parent in prison. The service is also committed to helping prisoners maintain their family ties. Good contact with the outside world helps prisoners to cope better inside prison and helps prepare them and their families for their return to the community. However, prisons are aware of the need to protect the well-being of the child, and Governors have the discretion to disallow any visit to an inmate by a person under 18 years of age if such a visit would not be in the best interest of the visitor. Similarly, a Governor has discretion to stop correspondence from a prisoner to a child if a parent requests it. Establishments are required to implement a range of measures to minimise the risk that certain prisoners, particularly those convicted of, or charged with, sexual offences against children may present to children. To ensure the safety of children when considering visits or other contact with convicted prisoners, Prison Governors are expected to seek and follow advice from social services departments, where necessary. When a social services department receives such a request for advice and considers it has the necessary powers under the Children Act 1989, it should assist the prison by assessing whether it is in the interests of a particular child to visit a named prisoner.

3.70 Where a prisoner is pregnant, or has a young baby, a multi-disciplinary team is responsible for assessing applications for placement on a mother and baby unit. The paramount concern is the best interests of the child. Parental responsibility for the care of a child in a mother and baby unit lies with the mother. The health and development of the child are monitored by a health visitor attached to the local NHS Trust. If there is concern about the care provided by the mother, this concern should always be reported and local social services informed, to consider how best to safeguard the child and promote his or her welfare. As a child grows older, prison becomes an increasingly unsuitable environment to enable normal child development: babies do not remain in mother and baby units beyond the age of 18 months.

3.71 The prison service has a duty to protect and promote the welfare of those children in its custody. Each prison service establishment which holds young people under 18 years of age is required to establish its own child protection committee, to appoint a child protection co-ordinator and to establish, in consultation with local ACPCs, a local child protection policy, detailing arrangements for acting on allegations or concerns that a young person may have suffered, or is at risk of suffering significant harm.

Youth Justice Services

3.72 The Crime and Disorder Act 1998, in its creation of Youth Offending Teams (YOTs) introduced an inter-agency approach to responding to children and young people involved in offending behaviour. The principal aim of youth justice services is to prevent offending through:

- a clear strategy to prevent offending and re-offending;
- helping offenders, and their parents, to face up to their offending and take responsibility for it;
- earlier, more effective intervention when young people first offend;
- faster, more efficient procedures from arrest to sentence; *and*
- partnership between all youth justice agencies to deliver a better, faster system.

The 1998 Act provides a range of powers to deal, in particular, with anti-social behaviour by the very young, with a view to diverting such children from crime. For those children and young people who have offended, there is a range of powers for the police and the courts to use when intervening.

3.73 Chief executives of local authorities with education and social services responsibilities take the lead in operating YOTs and preparing youth justice plans, in partnership with the police, probation service and health authorities. YOTs, like ACPCs (see para. 4.1) cover every local authority area, and will involve other agencies and organisations with relevant skills and experience. The YOTs are responsible for:

- co-ordinating the provision of youth justice services for those in the area who need them, as set out in the annual plan;
- carrying out the functions assigned to the Team, such as directly delivering services and ensuring the proper delivery of services by others; *and*
- undertaking to prevent offending.

3.74 A number of the children and young people who fall within the remit of YOTs will also be children in need, including some whose needs will include safeguarding. It is necessary, therefore, for there to be clear links, both at ACPC/YOT strategic level, as well as at child-specific operational level, between youth justice and child protection services. These links should be incorporated in each local authority's Children's Services Plan, the ACPC business plan and youth justice plan itself. At the operational level, protocols are likely to be of assistance in establishing cross-referral arrangements.

The Voluntary and Private Sectors

3.75 Voluntary organisations and private sector providers play an important role in children's services. In broad terms, their roles fall within the following areas:

Helplines: National helplines are now operated on a free 24 hour basis by both ChildLine and the National Society for the Prevention of Cruelty to Children (NSPCC). ChildLine's service is available for all children in trouble or in danger while the NSPCC's service exists primarily for adults who have concerns about children. In addition, Parentline is developing a national support helpline for parents under stress. All of these services, along with many other smaller helplines, provide important routes into statutory and voluntary services for children in need and for those whose needs include safeguarding from significant harm.

Provision of Direct Services: Both voluntary and private sector organisations provide a range of services for children and families. Their work is particularly central in the family support field and as the main providers of day care services. Other services include:

- advocacy projects for looked-after children and for parents and children who are the subject of s.47 enquiries and child protection conferences;
- providing independent persons and visitors;
- home visiting and befriending/support programmes;
- support to disabled children and their families including the provision of short-term breaks;
- services for children who are victims or witnesses of crime;
- specialist services for disabled children and those with health problems (e.g. interpreters for deaf children; information on rare medical conditions or disabilities; the provision or loan of specialist equipment);
- work in schools and other areas with peer support programmes;
- therapeutic work with children and families particularly in relation to child sexual abuse.

Public Education/Campaigning: Voluntary organisations fulfil a key role in providing information and resources to the wider public about the needs of children and resources to help families. A further important role fulfilled by the sector is that of advocacy, both in terms of individual cases and through campaigning on behalf of wider groups on specific issues. This often takes place through involvement in local ACPC activities.

3.76 While the NSPCC alone among voluntary organisations is authorised to initiate proceedings under the terms of the Children Act 1989, voluntary organisations undertake assessments of need and provide therapeutic and other services to children who have been abused. Such services are often provided within the context of child protection plans for children whose names are on the child protection register. The voluntary sector also makes a significant contribution to the development and provision of services for children abused through prostitution and for children who abuse other children.

3.77 The range of roles fulfilled by organisations from the voluntary and private sectors means that they need to have clear guidance and procedures in place to ensure appropriate referrals and co-operation with ACPC procedures. Staff and volunteers will need to be trained to be aware of the risks to and needs of children with whom they have contact.

Housing Authorities

3.78 Housing authorities can play an important role in safeguarding children in respect of recognition, referral and the subsequent management of risk. Housing authority staff, through their day to day contact with members of the public may become aware of concerns about the welfare of particular children and should refer to one of the statutory agencies in appropriate cases.

3.79 Equally, housing authorities may have important information about families that could be helpful to local authorities carrying out assessments under s.17 or s.47 of the Children Act 1989. In accordance with their duty to assist under s.27 of the Children Act 1989, they should be prepared to share relevant information orally or in writing, including attending child protection conferences when requested to do so.

3.80 Appropriate housing can make an important contribution to meeting the health and developmental needs of children, including those who need safeguarding from significant harm. Housing authorities should be prepared to assist by the provision of accommodation either directly, through their links with other housing providers, or by the provision of advice. Examples could include situations where women and children become homeless or at risk of homelessness as a result of domestic violence.

3.81 Housing authorities also have an important part to play in the management of the risk posed by dangerous offenders, including those who are assessed as presenting a risk, whether sexual or otherwise, to children. Appropriate housing can contribute greatly to the ability of the police and others to manage the risk such individuals pose.

Guardians Ad Litem

3.82 The *Guardian Ad Litem* and Reporting Officer (GALRO) service is currently provided by local authorities as a statutory responsibility. Its function in care and related proceedings under the Children Act 1989, and many proceedings under adoption legislation, is to safeguard and promote the interests of individual children who are the subject of the proceedings by providing independent social work advice to the court. In care-related applications where the child is a party to the proceedings, the *guardian ad litem* appoints a solicitor to represent the child and is responsible for instructing the solicitor.

3.83 The *guardian ad litem's* role as an officer of the court is limited to the duration of the court proceedings, including any appeal that might be lodged. In each case the *guardian ad litem* should exercise discretion over how best to undertake enquiries, assess information, consult a range of professionals and report to the court at interim hearings, directions appointments and at the final hearing.

3.84 The *guardian ad litem* has a statutory right to access and to take copies of local authority records which relate to the child concerned and any application under the Children Act 1989. That power also extends to other records which relate to the child and the wider functions of the local authority or records held by an authorised person (i.e. the NSPCC) which relate to that child.

3.85 An appointed *guardian ad litem* should always be invited to all formal planning meetings convened by the local authority in respect of the child. This includes statutory reviews of children who are accommodated or looked after and child protection conferences. The *guardian ad litem* may sometimes wish to attend such meetings to obtain information. The conference chair should ensure that all those attending such meetings, including in particular the child and any family members, understand that the *guardian ad litem's* presence does not imply any responsibility for decisions reached at such meetings.

3.86 The Government intends to set up a new service which will combine the present Family Court Welfare function provided by the Probation Service, the Children's Branch of the Official Solicitor's Department and the GALRO service which local authorities currently provide. The Lord Chancellor will take responsibility for the new service, which will be set up as a non-Departmental Public Body. The service will serve the Family Division of the High Court, County Courts, including care centres, and Family Proceedings courts.

The Wider Community

3.87 Everybody shares some responsibility for promoting the welfare of children, as a parent or family member, a concerned friend or neighbour, an employer, staff member or volunteer. Members of the community can help to safeguard children if they are mindful of children's needs, and willing and able to act if they have concerns about a child's welfare. Local agencies can do much to promote a partnership with families and the wider community by communicating openly with local people and the media about their work, and providing accessible information and advice in a form which is clear and relevant to all population groups. Relevant information might include details of the services local agencies provide, how and when to make contact where there are concerns about a child, and the response that members of the public and service users should expect. This will help people to develop a more informed understanding about when it would be appropriate to approach statutory agencies, how to do so, and when they may be eligible to receive a service. Statutory agencies can also help services run by community, religious and other voluntary groups, through providing advice and training on how to provide a safe service to children.

3.88 Members of communities also possess strengths and skills which can be harnessed for the benefit of vulnerable children and their families, including children at risk of significant harm. Community resources might include self-help and mutual aid initiatives, information resources and networks, support services, and advocacy and campaigning initiatives.

The Armed Services

3.89 The life of a Service family differs in many respects from that of a family in civilian life, particularly for those living overseas or on bases and garrisons in the UK, in housing provided by the Ministry of Defence (MoD). The Services control the movement of the family in response to Service commitments and the frequency of such moves makes it essential that the Service authorities are aware of any child for whom there are child protection concerns. The Armed Forces are fully committed to co-operating with statutory and other agencies in supporting families in this situation, and have in place procedures to help in safeguarding children. In areas of concentration of Service families, the Armed Forces seek particularly to work alongside local social services departments, including through representation on local ACPCs, and at child protection conferences.

3.90 Local authorities have the statutory responsibility for the protection of the children of Service families. All three Services provide professional welfare support including 'special to type' social work services and, in some cases, medical services to augment those provided by local authorities. In the Royal Navy (RN) this is provided by the Naval Personal and Family Service (NPFS) and the Royal Marines Welfare Service. Within the Army this is provided by the Army Welfare Service in partnership with Soldiers', Sailors', Air Force Association-Forces Help (SSAFA-FH) and in the Royal Air Force by SSAFA-FH. Further details of these services and contact numbers are given at Appendix 2.

3.91 When Service families (or civilians working with the Armed Forces) are based overseas, the responsibility for the protection of their children is vested with the MoD. The military authorities work in conjunction with the specialist authorities, particularly SSAFA-FH, who provide a fully qualified Social Work and Community Health service in major overseas locations (for example in Germany and Cyprus). Instructions for the protection of children overseas, which reflect the principles of the Children Act 1989 and the philosophy of inter-agency co-operation, are issued by the MoD as a 'Defence Council Instruction (Joint Service)' (DCI(JS)). Larger overseas Commands issue local child protection procedures, hold a Command Child Protection Register and have a Command Child Protection Committee which operates in a similar way to ACPCs in the UK in upholding standards and making sure that best practice is reflected in procedures and observed in practice.

Movement of Children to the United Kingdom from Overseas

3.92 When a Service family with a child who requires protection from significant harm is about to return to the UK, SSAFA-FH or the NPFS is responsible for informing the appropriate social services department and for ensuring that full documentation is provided to help in the management of the case.

3.93 When it appears that an application for an Emergency Protection Order (EPO) should be made in respect of a child overseas, a designated person may make an application for an EPO to a Commanding Officer. The grounds for making an Order mirror those for EPOs under the Children Act 1989 and are contained in sections 17–23 of the Armed Forces Act 1991. If, at a child protection conference, it is decided that it is not in the best interests of the child to return to the family home, the child will be placed in the care of an appropriate local authority social services department in the UK. Should this occur, the EPO made in the overseas

Command remains in effect for 24 hours following the arrival of the child in the UK. During this period, the local authority must decide whether to apply to the UK court for a further EPO. In such cases it is the duty of the responsible person (through the Service Authorities) to help parents to return to the UK so that they can be involved with all proceedings and decisions affecting their child.

Movement of Children from the United Kingdom to Overseas

3.94 Local authorities should ensure that SSAFA-FH (or the NPFS for RN families) is made aware of any Service child whose name is on a child protection register whose family is about to move overseas. In the interests of the child, SSAFA-FH/NPFS can confirm appropriate resources exist in the proposed location to meet identified needs. Full documentation should be provided which will be forwarded to the relevant overseas Command. All referrals should be made to the Director of Social Work, HQ SSAFA-FH or Area Officer, NPFS(East) (as appropriate) at the addresses given at Appendix 2.

United States Forces Stationed in the United Kingdom

3.95 Each local authority with an United States (US) base in its area should establish liaison arrangements with the base commander and relevant staff. The requirements of English child welfare legislation should be explained clearly to the US authorities, so that local authorities can fulfil their statutory duties.

Enquiries about Children of Ex-Service Families

3.96 Where a local authority believes that a child who is the subject of current child protection processes is from an ex-Service family, SSAFA-FH can be contacted to establish whether there is existing information which might help with enquiries. Enquiries should be addressed to the Director of Social Work, SSAFA-FH at the address given at Appendix 2.

Area Child Protection Committees

Role and Responsibilities

4.1 Local authorities, in exercising their social services functions, should ensure that there is an Area Child Protection Committee (ACPC) covering their area, which brings together representatives of each of the main agencies and professionals responsible for helping to protect children from abuse and neglect. The ACPC is an inter-agency forum for agreeing how the different services and professional groups should co-operate to safeguard children in that area, and for making sure that arrangements work effectively to bring about good outcomes for children.

4.2 The specific responsibilities of an ACPC are:

- to develop and agree local policies and procedures for inter-agency work to protect children, within the national framework provided by this guidance;

- to audit and evaluate how well local services work together to protect children, for example through wider case audits;

- to put in place objectives and performance indicators for child protection, within the framework and objectives set out in Children's Services Plans;

- to encourage and help develop effective working relationships between different services and professional groups, based on trust and mutual understanding;

- to ensure that there is a level of agreement and understanding across agencies about operational definitions and thresholds for intervention;

- to improve local ways of working in the light of knowledge gained through national and local experience and research, and to make sure that any lessons learned are shared, understood, and acted upon;

- to undertake case reviews where a child has died or – in certain circumstances – been seriously harmed, and abuse or neglect are confirmed or suspected. To make sure that any lessons from the case are understood and acted upon, to communicate clearly to individual services and professional groups their shared responsibility for protecting children, and to explain how each can contribute;

- to help improve the quality of child protection work and of inter-agency working through specifying needs for inter-agency training and development, and ensuring that training is delivered; *and*

- to raise awareness within the wider community of the need to safeguard children and promote their welfare and to explain how the wider community can contribute to these objectives.

Scope of Interest

4.3 The scope of the responsibilities outlined at paragraph 4.2 (above) should, as a minimum, extend to:

relevant population

- children abused and neglected within families, including those so harmed in the context of domestic violence;
- children abused outside families by adults known to them;
- children abused and neglected by professional carers, within an institutional setting, or anywhere else where children are cared for away from home;
- children abused by strangers;
- children abused by other young people;
- young perpetrators of abuse;
- children involved in prostitution; *and*
- children who misuse drugs and alcohol.

relevant activities

- raising awareness within the wider community, including faith and minority ethnic communities, and among statutory, voluntary and independent agencies, about how everybody can contribute to safeguarding children and promoting their welfare;
- working together across agencies to identify and act upon concerns about a child's safety and welfare; *and*
- working together across agencies to help those children who have suffered, or who are at continuing risk of significant harm, in order to safeguard such children and promote their welfare.

Accountability

4.4   ACPCs are accountable for their work to their main constituent agencies, whose agreement is required for all work which has implications for policy, planning and the allocation of resources. Programmes of work should be agreed and endorsed at a senior level within each of the main member agencies, within the framework of the children's services plan. The planned programme of work, and a report on progress the previous year should be set out in an annual business plan.

4.5   Each local authority with social services responsibility should take lead responsibility for the establishment and effective working of ACPCs, although all main constituent agencies are responsible for contributing fully and effectively to the work of the ACPC.

4.6   The Secretary of State for Health may seek comments or information from ACPCs on child protection matters from time to time.

ACPCs and Children's Services Planning

4.7   Each local authority with social services responsibilities is required to produce a children's services plan which should bring together all aspects of local services for children. Plans should look widely at the needs of local children, and the ways in which local services (including statutory and voluntary services) should work together to meet those needs. They should include specific priorities and proposals for improving children's services, and details of what action will be taken by whom and how the outcomes will be monitored.

4.8   The local authority as a whole should consider how all its services promote the welfare of children. This includes the contribution which can be made by education, social services, housing, youth services, culture, leisure and other departments. Other services should work in partnership with local authorities to produce local children's services plans, especially the health service and youth justice services (including police and probation). The outcome should be a plan to which all local services are signed up and committed to putting into effect.

4.9 ACPCs should contribute to, and work within the framework established by the children's services plan. ACPCs should have a clear role in identifying those children in need who are at risk of significant harm, or who have suffered significant harm, and in identifying resource gaps (in terms of funding and/or the contribution of different agencies) and better ways of working. Within the children's services planning framework, different services will also work together in different forums to plan co-ordinated action in areas relevant to children and child protection. Examples include early years development, substance misuse, domestic violence, youth offending, and improving public health. The children's services plan should make links between these related activities. Informed by the plan, the ACPC should be aware of and contribute to the work of others, and vice-versa.

ACPC Membership

4.10 To carry out their responsibilities effectively, ACPCs should have members from each of the main agencies responsible for working together to safeguard children, whose roles and seniority enable them to contribute to developing and maintaining strong and effective inter-agency child protection procedures and protocols, and ensure that local child protection services are adequately resourced.

4.11 Membership should be determined locally, but should include as a minimum representation from:

- local authorities (education and social services);
- health services (covering both managerial and professional expertise and responsibilities);
- the police;
- the probation service;
- NSPCC (when active in the area);
- the domestic violence forum (when active in the area);
- the armed services (where appropriate, and especially where there is a large service base in the area).

4.12 The ACPC should make appropriate arrangements to involve others in its work as needed. Those with a relevant interest may include (the following list is not intended to be comprehensive):

- adult mental health services, including forensic mental health services;
- child and adolescent mental health services;
- the coroner;
- the Crown Prosecution Service;
- dental health services;
- drug and alcohol misuse services;
- education establishments not maintained by the local authority;
- *Guardian Ad Litem* panels;
- housing, cultural and leisure services;
- the judiciary;
- local authority legal services;

- prisons and youth detention centres;
- representatives of service users;
- representatives of foster carers;
- sexual health services;
- voluntary agencies providing help to parents and children;
- witness support services; *and*
- Youth Offending Teams.

4.13 Many ACPCs have found it useful to set up working groups or sub-groups, on a short-term or a standing basis:

- to carry out specific tasks (e.g. maintaining and updating procedures and protocols; reviewing serious cases; identifying inter-agency training needs and arranging appropriate training);
- to provide specialist advice (e.g. in respect of working with specific ethnic or cultural groups, or with disabled children and/or parents);
- to represent a defined geographical area within the ACPC's boundaries.

4.14 All groups working under the auspices of the ACPC should have been established by the ACPC, and work to agreed terms of reference within the framework of the annual business plan, with explicit lines of reporting, communication and accountability to the ACPC.

Ways of Working

Chairing

4.15 The ACPC should be chaired by somebody of sufficient standing and expertise to command the respect and support of member agencies, and who has a firm grasp of local operational issues. The chair may come from any member agency, chairing may rotate between member agencies, or the chair may be independent of member agencies according to local decision.

Financing and Administration

4.16 ACPC expenditure, and administrative and policy support, is a matter for local agreement. As a multi-agency forum, the ACPC should be supported in its work by its main constituent agencies, reflecting the investment of each agency in activities which are of benefit to all, in particular inter-agency training.

ACPC Boundaries

4.17 Where boundaries between local authorities, the health service and the police are not co-terminous, there can be problems for some member agencies in having to work to different procedures and protocols according to the area involved, or in having to participate in several ACPCs. It may be helpful in these circumstances for an ACPC to cover an area which includes more than one local authority area, or for adjoining ACPCs to collaborate as far as possible on establishing common procedures and protocols and on inter-agency training.

ACPC Protocols

4.18 This guidance asks ACPCs to have in place local protocols covering:

- how s.47 enquiries and associated police investigations should be conducted, and in particular, in what circumstances joint enquiries are necessary and/or appropriate;

- quick and straightforward means of resolving professional differences of view in a specific case, e.g. on whether a child protection conference should be convened;

- attendance at child protection conferences, including quora;

- involving children and family members in child protection conferences, the role of advocates as well as including criteria for excluding parents in exceptional circumstances;

- a decision-making process for registration based upon the views of the agencies present at the child protection conference;

- handling complaints from families about the functioning of child protection conferences (see paras. 5.71–5.73); *and*

- responding to children involved in prostitution.

Annual Business Plans

4.19 Each ACPC should produce an annual business plan, setting out a work programme for the forthcoming year, including measurable objectives; relevant management information on child protection activity in the course of the previous year; and progress against objectives the previous year. ACPC plans should both contribute to and derive from the framework of the local children's services plan and should be endorsed by senior managers in each of the main constituent agencies.

4.20 ACPCs are encouraged to make the business plan, or an edited version of it, available to a wider audience, for example to explain to the wider community the work of local agencies in helping to keep children safe and thriving.

5

Handling individual cases

Introduction

5.1   This section provides advice on what should happen if somebody has concerns about the welfare of a child (including those living away from home), together with concerns that a child may be suffering, or at risk of suffering, abuse or neglect. It is not intended as a detailed practice guide, but it sets out clear expectations about the ways in which agencies and professionals should work together in the interests of children's safety and well-being.

Being Alert to Children's Welfare

5.2   Everybody who works with children, parents, and other adults in contact with children should be able to recognise, and know how to act upon, indicators that a child's welfare or safety may be at risk. Professionals, foster carers, staff members and managers should be mindful always of the welfare and safety of children – including unborn children and older children – in their work:

With children

for example: teachers, school nurses, health visitors, GPs, Accident and Emergency and all other hospital staff should be able to recognise possible indicators of abuse or neglect in children, or situations where a child requires extra support to prevent significant impairment to his or her health or development;

With parents or carers who may need help in promoting and safeguarding their children's welfare

for example: adult mental health or substance misuse services should always consider the implications for children of patients' or users' problems. Day nurseries and family centres should keep the interests of children uppermost when working with parents, work in ways intended to bring about better outcomes for children, and be alert to possible indicators of abuse or neglect. When dealing with cases of domestic violence, the police and other involved agencies should consider the implications of the situation for any children in the family;

With family members, employees, or others who have contact with children

for example: the police and probation services, mental health services, and housing authorities should be alert to the possibility that an individual may pose a risk of harm to a particular child, or to children in a local community. Employers of staff or volunteers who have substantial unsupervised access to children should guard against the potential for abuse, through rigorous selection processes, appropriate supervision and by taking steps to maintain a safe environment for children.

5.3 A professional or staff member who may encounter concerns about the well-being or safety of a child or children should know:

- what services are available locally, how to gain access to them;
- what sources of further advice and expertise are available, who to contact in what circumstances, and how; *and*
- when and how to make a referral to the local authority social services department.

5.4 Sources of information and advice should include at least one designated senior doctor and nurse within each health authority area, and a designated teacher within each school. There should always be the opportunity to discuss child welfare concerns with, and seek advice from, colleagues, managers, a designated or named professional, or other agencies, but:

- never delay emergency action to protect a child;
- always record in writing concerns about a child's welfare, whether or not further action is taken;
- always record in writing discussions about a child's welfare. At the close of a discussion, always reach clear and explicit recorded agreement about who will be taking what action, or that no further action will be taken.

Referrals to Social Services Departments Where There Are Child Welfare Concerns

5.5 Social services departments have responsibilities towards all children whose health or development may be impaired without the provision of support and services, or who are disabled (described by the Children Act 1989 as children 'in need'). Social services departments should let families know how to contact them and what they might expect by way of help, advice and services. They should agree criteria with other local services and professionals as to when it is appropriate to make a referral to social services departments in respect of a child in need.

5.6 If somebody believes that a child may be suffering, or may be at risk of suffering significant harm, then s/he should always refer his or her concerns to the local authority social services department. In addition to the social services department, the police and the NSPCC have powers to intervene in these circumstances. Sometimes concerns will arise within the social services department itself, as new information comes to light about a child and family with whom the service is already in contact. While professionals should seek, in general, to discuss any concerns with the family and, where possible, seek their agreement to making referrals to social services, **this should only be done where such discussion and agreement-seeking will not place a child at increased risk of significant harm.**

5.7 When a parent, professional, or another person contacts a social services department with concerns about a child's welfare, it is the responsibility of the social services department to clarify with the referrer (including self-referrals from families): the nature of concerns; how and why they have arisen; and what appear to be the needs of the child and family. This process should always identify clearly whether there are concerns about abuse or neglect, what is their foundation, and whether the child/ren may need urgent action to make them safe from harm.

5.8 Whenever the social services department (or the NSPCC if relevant) encounters or has a case referred to it which constitutes, or may constitute, a criminal offence against a child, it should always inform the police at the earliest opportunity. This will enable both agencies to consider jointly how to proceed in the best interests of the child. In dealing with alleged offences involving a child victim, the police should normally work in partnership with social services and/or other child welfare agencies. Whilst the responsibility to instigate criminal proceedings rests with the police, they should consider the views expressed by other agencies. There will be less serious cases where, after discussion, it is agreed that the best interests of the child are served by social services led intervention rather than a full police investigation.

5.9 Professionals who phone the social services department should confirm referrals in writing. At the end of any discussion or dialogue about a child, the referrer (whether a professional or a member of the public or family) and the social services department should be clear about who will be taking what action, or that no further action will be taken. The decision should be recorded by the social services department, and by the referrer (if a professional in another service).

5.10 The social services department should decide on the next course of action within 24 hours, normally following discussion with any referring professional/service, looking at any existing records, and involving other professionals and services as necessary (including the police, where a criminal offence may have been committed against a child). This initial consideration of the case should address – on the basis of the available evidence – whether there are concerns about either the child's health and development, or actual and/or potential harm which justify further enquiries, assessment and/or intervention. If further action is needed, a decision is needed on when enquiries and/or intervention should take place.

5.11 Parents' permission should be sought before discussing a referral about them with other agencies, unless permission-seeking may itself place a child at risk of significant harm. When responding to referrals from the wider community, it should be borne in mind that personal information about referrers, including identifying details, should only be disclosed to third parties (including subject families and other agencies) with the consent of the referrer. In all cases where the police are involved, the decision about when to inform the parents (about referrals from third parties) will have a bearing on the conduct of police investigations.

5.12 Referrals may lead to no further action, directly to the provision of services or other help – including from other agencies – and/or to a fuller initial assessment of the needs and circumstances of the child which may, in turn, be followed by s.47 enquiries. Where social services decides to take no further action at this stage, feedback should be provided to the referrer. In the case of public referrals, this should be done in a manner consistent with respecting the confidentiality of the child. Sometimes it may be apparent at this stage that emergency action should be taken to safeguard a child (see para. 5.23). Such action should normally be preceded by an immediate strategy discussion between the police, social services and other agencies as appropriate.

Initial Assessment

5.13 The initial assessment by the social services department of all children in need – whether or not there are child protection concerns – should be completed within a maximum of seven working days of the date of referral. However, the initial assessment period may be very brief if the criteria for initiating s.47 enquiries are met. Using the framework set out in the *Framework for the Assessment of Children in Need and their Families* it should address the questions:

* what are the needs of the child?
* are the parents able to respond appropriately to the child's needs? Is the child being adequately safeguarded from significant harm, and are the parents able to promote the child's health and development?
* is action required to safeguard and promote the child's welfare?

5.14 The process of initial assessment should involve: seeing and speaking to the child (according to age and understanding) and family members as appropriate; drawing together and analysing available information from a range of sources (including existing records); and obtaining relevant information from professionals and others in contact with the child and family. All relevant information (including historical information) should be taken into account.

5.15 In the course of this assessment, the social services department should ask:

- is this a child in need? (s.17 of the Children Act 1989)
- is there reasonable cause to suspect that this child is suffering, or is likely to suffer, significant harm? (s.47 of the Children Act 1989).

5.16 The focus of the initial assessment should be the welfare of the child. It is important to remember that even if the reason for a referral was a concern about abuse or neglect

Section 17(1) of the Children Act 1989 states that:

It shall be the general duty of every local authority (in addition to the other duties imposed on them by this Part) -

a) to safeguard and promote the welfare of children within their area who are in need; and

b) so far as is consistent with that duty, to promote the upbringing of such children by their families, by providing a range and level of services appropriate to those children's needs.

Section 17(10) states that a child shall be taken to be in need if:

a) he is unlikely to achieve or maintain, or to have the opportunity of achieving or maintaining, a reasonable standard of health or development without the provision for him of services by a local authority under this Part;

b) his health or development is likely to be significantly impaired, or further impaired, without the provision of such services; or

c) he is disabled.

Section 47(1) of the Children Act 1989 states that:

Where a local authority -

a) are informed that a child who lives, or is found, in their area -
   i) is the subject of an emergency protection order; or
   ii) is in police protection; or
   iii) has contravened a ban imposed by a curfew notice imposed within the meaning of Chapter I of Part I of the Crime and Disorder Act 1998; or

b) have reasonable cause to suspect that a child who lives, or is found, in their area is suffering, or is likely to suffer, significant harm, the authority shall make, or cause to be made, such enquiries as they consider necessary to enable them to decide whether they should take any action to safeguard or promote the child's welfare.

In the case of a child falling within paragraph (a)(iii) above, the enquiries shall be commenced as soon as practicable and, in any event, within 48 hours of the authority receiving the information.

which is not subsequently substantiated, a family may still benefit from support and practical help to promote a child's health and development.

5.17 Following an initial assessment, the social services department should decide on the next course of action, following discussion with the child and family, unless such a discussion may place a child at risk of significant harm. Where it is clear that there should be a police investigation in parallel with a s.47 enquiry, the considerations at para. 5.36 should apply. Whatever decisions are taken, they should be endorsed at a managerial level agreed within the social services department and recorded in writing, with the reasons for them. The family, the original referrer, and other professionals and services involved in the assessment, should as far as possible be told what action has been taken, consistent with respecting the confidentiality of the child and family concerned, and not jeopardising further action in respect of child protection concerns (which may include police investigations).

Initial Assessment and Enquiries Where There Are Child Protection Concerns – What Research Tells Us

5.18 A review of relevant research was published in 1998 to disseminate current child abuse research findings relevant to an initial visit to a family in a child protection enquiry. In conducting their review, the researchers identified ten common pitfalls as revealed in the research, and made recommendations on how to avoid them[2].

5.19 These pitfalls and advice on how to avoid them are presented in summary form – as summarised by the researchers – on the following page. This research based information is intended to assist, not to replace professional judgement during an initial assessment (and any subsequent s.47 enquiries or alternatively any subsequent s.47 enquiries).

Next Steps – No Suspected Actual or Likely Significant Harm

5.20 An initial assessment may indicate that a child may be 'in need' as defined by s.17 of the Children Act 1989, but that there are no substantiated concerns that the child may be suffering, or at risk of suffering significant harm. In these circumstances, the *Framework for the Assessment of Children in Need and their Families* provides a framework for a core assessment of a child's health and development, and the parents' capacity to respond to their child's needs. This core assessment can provide a sound evidence base for professional judgements on whether services would be helpful to a child and family, and if so, types of service is most likely to bring about good outcomes for the child. Family Group Conferences (see paras. 7.13–7.18) may be an effective vehicle for taking forward work in such cases.

5.21 The definition of a 'child in need' is wide, and it will embrace children in a diverse range of circumstances. The types of services which may help such children and their families will vary greatly according to their needs and circimstances.

> The rest of the guidance in this chapter is concerned with the processes which should be followed where a child is suspected to be suffering, or likely to suffer, significant harm.

---

2. Cleaver H, Wattam C, Cawson P, Gordon R. *Children Living at Home: The Initial Child Protection Enquiry. Ten Pitfalls and How to Avoid Them*. In: *Assessing Risk in Child Protection*. London: NSPCC, 1998.

Initial assessment and enquiries: Ten pitfalls and how to avoid them

1. Not enough weight is given to information from family, friends and neighbours.

Ask yourself: Would I react differently if these reports had come from a different source? How can I check whether or not they have substance? Even if they are not accurate, could they be a sign that the family are inneed of some help or support?

2. Not enough attention is paid to what children say, how they look and how they behave.

Ask yourself: Have I been given appropriate access to all the children in the family? If I have not been able to see any child, is there a very good reason, and have I made arrangements to see him/her as soon as possible, or made sure that another relevant professional sees him/her? How should I follow up any uneasiness about the child/ren's health or well-being? If the child is old enough and has the communication skills, what is the child's account of events? If the child uses a language other than English, or alternative non verbal communication, have I made every effort to enlist help in understanding him/her? What is the evidence to support or refute the young person's account?

3. Attention is focused on the most visible or pressing problems and other warning signs are not appreciated.

Ask yourself: What is the most striking thing about this situation? If this feature were to be removed or changed, would I still have concerns?

4. Pressures from high status referrers or the press, with fears that a child may die, lead to over-precipitate action.

Ask yourself: Would I see this referral as a child protection matter if it came from another source?

5. Professionals think that when they have explained something as clearly as they can, the other person will have understood it.

Ask yourself: Have I double-checked with the family and the child/ren that they understand what will happen next?

6. Assumptions and pre-judgements about families lead to observations being ignored or misinterpreted.

Ask yourself: What were my assumptions about this family? What, if any, is the hard evidence which supports them? What, if any, is the hard evidence which refutes them?

7. Parents' behaviour, whether co-operative or unco-operative, is often misinterpreted.

Ask yourself: What were the reasons for the parents' behaviour? Are there other possibilities besides the most obvious? Could their behaviour have been a reaction to something I did or said rather than to do with the child?

8. When the initial enquiry shows that the child is not at risk of significant harm, families are seldom referred to other services which they need to prevent longer term problems.

Ask yourself: Is this family's situation satisfactory for meeting the child/ren's needs? Whether or not there is a child protection concern, does the family need support or practical help? How can I make sure they know about services they are entitled to, and can access them if they wish?

9. When faced with an aggressive or frightening family, professionals are reluctant to discuss fears for their own safety and ask for help.

Ask yourself: Did I feel safe in this household? If not, why not? If I or another professional should go back there to ensure the child/ren's safety, what support should I ask for? If necessary, put your concerns and requests in writing to your manager.

10. Information taken at the first enquiry is not adequately recorded, facts are not checked and reasons for decisions are not noted.

Ask yourself: Am I sure the information I have noted is 100% accurate? If I didn't check my notes with the family during the interview, what steps should I take to verify them? Do my notes show clearly the difference between the information the family gave me, my own direct observations, and my interpretation or assessment of the situation? Do my notes record what action I have taken/will take? What action all other relevant people have taken/will take?

Next Steps – Suspected Actual or Likely Significant Harm

5.22   Where a child is suspected to be suffering, or likely to suffer, significant harm, local authority social services departments are required by s.47 of the Children Act 1989 to make enquiries, to enable the local authority to decide whether it should take any action to safeguard or promote the child's welfare. The *Framework for the Assessment of Children in Need and their Families* is equally relevant in these circumstances as a structured framework for collecting, drawing together and analysing available information about a child and family. It will help provide sound evidence on which to base often difficult professional judgements about whether to intervene to safeguard a child and promote his or her welfare and, if so, how best to do so and with what intended outcomes.

Immediate Protection

5.23   Where there is a risk to the life of a child or a likelihood of serious immediate harm, an agency with statutory child protection powers[3] **should act quickly to secure the immediate safety of the child.** Emergency action might be necessary as soon as a referral is received, or at any point in involvement with children and families. The need for emergency action may become apparent only over time as more is learned about the circumstances of a child or children. Neglect, as well as abuse, can pose such a risk of significant harm to a child that urgent protective action is needed. When considering whether emergency action is necessary, an agency should always consider whether action is also required to safeguard other children in the same household (e.g. siblings), the household of an alleged perpetrator, or elsewhere.

5.24   Planned emergency action will normally take place following an immediate strategy discussion between police, social services, and other agencies as appropriate (including NSPCC where involved). Where a single agency has to act immediately to protect a child, a strategy discussion should take place as soon as possible after such action to plan next steps. Legal advice should normally be obtained before initiating legal action, in particular when an Emergency Protection Order is to be sought.

5.25   In some cases, it may be sufficient to secure a child's safety by a parent taking action to remove an alleged perpetrator or by the alleged perpetrator agreeing to leave the home. In other cases, it may be necessary to ensure either that the child remains in a safe place or that the child is removed to a safe place, either on a voluntary basis or by obtaining an emergency protection order. The police also have powers to remove a child to suitable accommodation in cases of emergency. If it is necessary to remove a child, a local authority should wherever possible – and unless a child's safety is otherwise at immediate risk – apply for an emergency protection order, and should not seek to use police protection powers for this purpose.

5.26   The local authority in whose area a child is found, in circumstances that require emergency action, is responsible for taking that action. If the child is looked after by, or on the child protection register of, another authority, the first authority should consult the authority responsible for the child. Only if the looking after or registering local authority explicitly accepts responsibility is the first authority relieved of the responsibility to take emergency action. Such acceptance should be confirmed in writing.

5.27   Emergency action addresses only the immediate circumstances of the child(ren). It should be followed quickly by s.47 enquiries as necessary. The agencies primarily involved with the child and family should then assess the circumstances of the child

---

3. Agencies with statutory child protection powers comprise the local authority, the police, and the NSPCC.

Exclusion Orders

There are a range of powers available under the Family Law Act 1996 which may allow a perpetrator to be removed from the home, instead of having to remove the child. For the court to include an exclusion requirement in an order, it must be satisfied that:

- there is reasonable cause to believe that if the person is excluded from the home in which the child lives, the child will cease to suffer, or cease to be likely to suffer, significant harm; *and*

- another person living in the home is able and willing to give the child the care which it would be reasonable to expect a parent to give, and consents to the exclusion requirement.

Emergency Protection Orders

The court may make an emergency protection order under s.44 of the Children Act 1989 if it is satisfied that there is reasonable cause to believe that a child is likely to suffer significant harm if:

- he is not removed to accommodation; *or*

- he does not remain in the place in which he is then being accommodated.

An emergency protection order may also be made if s.47 enquiries are being frustrated by access to the child being unreasonably refused to a person authorised to seek access, and the applicant has reasonable cause to believe that access is needed as a matter of urgency.

An emergency protection order gives authority to remove a child, and places the child under the protection of the applicant for a maximum of eight days (with a possible extension of up to seven days).

Police Protection Powers

Under s.46 of the Children Act 1989, where a police officer has reasonable cause to believe that a child would otherwise be likely to suffer significant harm, s/he may:

- remove the child to suitable accommodation and keep him or her there; *or*

- take reasonable steps to ensure that the child's removal from any hospital, or other place in which the child is then being accommodated is prevented.

No child may be kept in police protection for more than 72 hours.

and family, and agree action to safeguard the child in the longer-term and to promote his or her welfare. Where an emergency protection order applies, the social services department needs to consider quickly whether to initiate care or other proceedings, or to let the order lapse and the child return home.

Strategy Discussion

5.28   Whenever there is reasonable cause to suspect that a child is suffering, or is likely to suffer significant harm, there should be a strategy discussion involving the social services department and the police, and other agencies as appropriate (e.g. education and health), in particular any referring agency. A strategy discussion may take place following a referral, or at any other time (e.g. if concerns about significant harm emerge in respect of child receiving support under s.17). Where a medical examination may be needed, a senior doctor from the providing service should be included in the strategy discussion. The discussion should be used to:

- share available information;
- decide whether s.47 enquiries should be initiated or continued if they have already begun;
- plan how enquiries should be handled, including the need for a medical treatment, and by whom;
- agree what action is needed immediately to safeguard the child, and/or provide interim services and support; *and*
- determine what information about the strategy discussion will be shared with the family, unless such information sharing may place a child at risk of significant harm or jeopardise police investigations into any alleged offence(s).

5.29 Relevant matters will include:

- agreeing a plan for s.47 enquiries as part of the core assessment – what further information is needed about the child/ren and family and how it should be obtained;
- agreeing who should be interviewed, by whom, for what purpose, and when. The way in which interviews are conducted can play a significant part in minimising any distress caused to children, and increasing the likelihood of maintaining constructive working relationships with families. When a criminal offence may have been committed against a child, the timing and handling of interviews with victims, their families and witnesses, can have important implications for the collection and preservation of evidence;
- in the light of the race and ethnicity of the child and family, considering how this should be taken into account in enquiries, and establishing whether an interpreter will be needed; *and*
- considering the needs of other children who may affected e.g. siblings and other children in contact with alleged abusers.

5.30 A strategy discussion may take place at a meeting or by other means (e.g. by telephone). Any information shared, all decisions reached, and the basis for those decisions, should be clearly recorded by all parties to the discussion.

5.31 Significant harm to children gives rise to both child welfare concerns and law enforcement concerns, and s.47 enquiries may run concurrently with police investigations concerning possible associated crime(s). The police have a duty to carry out thorough and professional investigations into allegations of crime, and the obtaining of clear strong evidence is in the best interests of a child, since it makes it less likely that a child victim will have to give evidence in criminal court. Enquiries may, therefore, give rise to information which is relevant to decisions which have to be taken by both the social services department and the police. They need to create the basis for future support and help to the child and family on a planned, co-ordinated basis. They may contribute to legal proceedings, whether criminal, civil or both.

5.32 Each ACPC should have in place a protocol for social services departments and the police, to guide both agencies in deciding how s.47 enquiries and associated police investigations should be conducted, and in particular, in what circumstances s.47 enquiries and linked criminal investigation are necessary and/or appropriate.

S.47 Enquiries and Core Assessment

5.33 The objective of local authority enquiries conducted under s.47 is to determine whether action is needed to promote and safeguard the welfare of the child or children who are the subject of the enquiries. The *Framework for the Assessment of Children in Need and their Families* provides a structure for helping to collect and analyse information obtained in the course of s.47 enquiries. Those making enquiries should always be alert to the potential needs and safety of any siblings, or other children in the household of the child in question. In addition, enquiries may also need to cover children in other households, with whom the alleged offender may have had contact. At the same time, the police will need (where relevant) to establish the facts about any offence which may have been committed against a child, and to collect evidence.

5.34 Assessing the needs of a child and the capacity of their parents or wider family network adequately to ensure their safety, health, and development, very often depends on building a picture of the child's situation on the basis of information from many sources. Enquiries should always involve separate interviews with the child who is the subject of concern and – in the great majority of cases – interviews with parents and/or carers, and observation of the interactions between parents and child/ren. Enquiries may also include interviews with those who are personally and professionally connected with the child; specific examinations or assessments of the child by other professionals (e.g. medical or developmental checks, assessment of emotional or psychological state); and interviews with those who are personally and professionally connected with the child's parents and/or carers.

5.35 Individuals should always be enabled to participate fully in the enquiry process. Where a child or parent is disabled, it may be necessary to provide help with communication to enable the child or parent to express him/herself to the best of his or her ability. Where a child or parent speaks a language other than that spoken by the interviewer, there should be an interpreter provided. If the child is unable to take part in an interview because of age or understanding, alternative means of understanding the child's perspective should be used, including observation where children are very young or where they have communication impairments.

5.36 Children are a key, and sometimes the only, source of information about what has happened to them, especially in child sexual abuse cases, but also in physical and other forms of abuse. Accurate and complete information is essential for taking action to promote the welfare of the child, as well as for any criminal proceedings which may be instigated concerning an alleged perpetrator of abuse. When children are first approached, the nature and extent of any harm suffered by them may not be clear, nor whether a criminal offence has been committed. It is important that even initial discussions with children are conducted in a way that minimises any distress caused to them, and maximises the likelihood that they will provide accurate and complete information. It is important, wherever possible, to have separate communication with a child. Leading or suggestive communication should always be avoided. Children may need time, and more than one opportunity, in order to develop sufficient trust to communicate any concerns they may have, especially if they have communication difficulties, learning difficulties, are very young, or are experiencing mental health problems.

5.37 Exceptionally, a joint enquiries/investigation team may need to speak to a suspected child victim without the knowledge of the parent or carer. Relevant circumstances would include the possibility that a child would be threatened or otherwise coerced into silence; a strong likelihood that important evidence would be destroyed; or that the child in question did not wish the parent to be involved at that stage, and is competent to take that decision. As at para. 5.11 above, in all cases where the police are involved, the decision about when to inform the parent or carer will have a bearing on the conduct of police investigations, and the strategy discussion should decide on the most appropriate timing of parental participation.

5.38 The Children Act 1989 places a statutory duty on health, education and other services, to help social services departments with their enquiries. The professionals conducting enquiries should do their utmost to secure willing co-operation and participation from all professionals and services, by being prepared to explain and justify their actions, and to demonstrate that the process is being managed in a way which can help to bring about better outcomes for children. The ACPC has an important role to play in cultivating and promoting a climate of trust and understanding between different professionals and services.

Investigative Interviews of Children

5.39 Sometimes there will be a need for an investigative interview, with a view to gathering evidence for criminal proceedings. A child should never be interviewed in the presence of an alleged or suspected perpetrator of abuse, or somebody who may be colluding with a perpetrator. The *Memorandum of Good Practice*[4] should be followed as a recognised good practice guide for all videoed investigative interviews with children.

5.40 All such interviews with children should be conducted by those with specialist training and experience in interviewing children. Additional specialist help may be needed if the child's first language is not English; the child appears to have a degree of psychiatric disturbance but is deemed competent; the child has an impairment; or where interviewers do not have adequate knowledge and understanding of the child's racial, religious or cultural background. Consideration should also be given to the gender of interviewers, particularly in cases of alleged sexual abuse.

5.41 Criminal justice legislation, in particular the Youth Justice and Criminal Evidence Act 1999, creates particular obligations for Courts who are dealing with witnesses under 17 years of age. These include the presumption of evidence-giving through pre-recorded videos, as well as the use of live video links for further evidence-giving and cross-examination. Cross-examination in pre-trial video hearings may also occur in relevant cases.

Child Assessment Orders

5.42 The local authority should make all reasonable efforts to persuade parents to co-operate with s.47 enquiries. If, despite these efforts, the parents continue to refuse access to a child for the purpose of establishing basic facts about the child's condition – but concerns about the child's safety are not so urgent as to require an emergency protection order – a local authority may apply to the court for a child assessment order. In these circumstances, the court may direct the parents/carers to co-operate with an assessment of the child, the details of which should be specified. The order does not take away the child's own right to refuse to participate in an assessment, e.g. a medical examination, so long as he or she is of sufficient age and understanding.

The Impact of Enquiries on the Family and Child

5.43 Enquiries should always be carried out in such a way as to minimise distress to the child, and to ensure that families are treated sensitively and with respect. The social services

4. *Memorandum of Good Practice on Video Recorded Interviews With Child Witnesses For Criminal Proceedings.* London: HMSO, 1992.

department should explain the purpose and outcome of s.47 enquiries to the parents and child (having regard to age and understanding) and be prepared to answer questions openly, unless to do so would affect the safety and welfare of the child. It is particularly helpful for families if social services departments provide written information about the purpose, process and potential outcomes of s.47 enquiries. The information should be both general and specific to the particular circumstances under enquiry. It should include information about how advice, advocacy and support may be obtained from independent sources.

5.44   In the great majority of cases, children remain with their families following enquiries, even where concerns about abuse or neglect are substantiated. As far as possible, enquiries should be conducted in a way which allows for future constructive working relationships with families. The way in which a case is handled initially can affect the entire subsequent process. Where handled well and sensitively, there can be a positive effect on the eventual outcome for the child.

The Outcome of S.47 Enquiries

5.45   The social services department should decide how to proceed following s.47 enquiries, after discussion between all those who have conducted, or been significantly involved in those enquiries, including relevant professionals and agencies, as well as foster carers where involved, and the child and parents themselves. The outcome of s.47 enquiries should be recorded and parents (together with professionals and agencies who have been significantly involved) should receive a copy of this record, in particular in advance of any initial child conference that is convened. It may be valuable, following an evaluation of the outcome of enquiries, to make recommendations for action in an inter-disciplinary forum, if the case is not going forward to a child protection conference. Enquiries may result in a number of outcomes.

Concerns are not Substantiated

5.46   Enquiries may not substantiate the original concerns about the child being at risk of, or suffering, significant harm. In these circumstances, no further action may be necessary. However, the social services department, and other relevant agencies as necessary, should always consider with the family whether there is a need for support and/or services; how the child and family might be provided with help, if they wish it; and by whom. The focus of child protection enquiries is the welfare of the child, and enquiries may well reveal a range of needs. A great many children who are the subject of child protection enquiries will fall within the definition of 'children in need'. The provision of help to these children and their families should not be dependent on the presence of abuse and neglect. Help and support to children in need and their families may help avoid problems developing into abuse or neglect.

5.47   In some cases, there may remain concerns about significant harm, but no real evidence. It may be appropriate to put in place arrangements to monitor the child's welfare (e.g. through a health visitor or school). Monitoring should never be used as a means of deferring or avoiding difficult decisions. The purpose of monitoring should always be clear, i.e. what is being monitored and why, in what way and by whom. It will also be important to inform parents about the nature of any on-going concern. There should be a time set for reviewing the monitoring arrangements through the holding a further discussion or meeting.

Concerns are Substantiated, but the Child is not Judged to be at Continuing Risk of Significant Harm

5.48   There may be substantiated concerns that a child has suffered significant harm, but it is agreed between the agencies most involved and the child and family, that a plan for ensuring the child's future safety and welfare can be developed and implemented without the need for a child protection conference or a child protection plan. Such an approach will be of particular relevance where it is clear to the agencies involved that there is no continuing risk of significant harm.

5.49 A child protection conference may not be required when there are sound reasons, based on an analysis of evidence obtained through enquiries, for judging that a child is not at continuing risk of significant harm. This may be because circumstances have changed, for example, if a perpetrator of abuse has permanently left the household. It may be because significant harm was incurred as the result of an isolated abusive incident (e.g. abuse by a stranger).

5.50 The agencies most involved may judge that a parent, carer, or members of the child's wider family are willing and able to co-operate with actions to ensure the child's future safety and well-being and that the child is therefore not at continuing risk of significant harm. This judgement can only be made in the light of all relevant information obtained during enquiries, and a soundly based assessment of the likelihood of successful intervention, based on clear evidence and mindful of the dangers of misplaced professional optimism. It is important to seek children's views and take account of their wishes and feelings, according to their age and understanding. In these circumstances, a meeting of involved professionals and family members may, nonetheless, be useful to agree what actions should be undertaken by whom, and with what intended outcomes for the child's safety and development, including the provision of therapeutic services. Whatever process is used to plan future action, the resulting plan should be informed by the assessment findings. It should set out who will have responsibility for what actions, including what course of action should be followed if the plan is not being successfully implemented. It should also include a timescale for review of progress against intended outcomes. Family Group Conferences (paras. 7.13–7.18) may have a role to play in fulfilling these tasks.

5.51 The social services department should take carefully any decision not to proceed to a child protection conference where it is known that a child has suffered significant harm. A suitably qualified and designated person within the social services department should endorse the decision. Those professionals and agencies who are most involved with the child and family, and those who have taken part in enquiries, have the right to request that social services convene a child protection conference if they have serious concerns that a child may not otherwise be adequately safeguarded. Any such request which is supported by a senior manager, or a named or designated professional, should normally be agreed. Where there remain differences of view over the need for a conference in a specific case, every effort should be made to resolve them through discussion and explanation, but as a last resort ACPCs should have in place a quick and straightforward means of resolving differences of opinion.

Concerns are Substantiated and the Child is Judged to be at Continuing Risk of Significant Harm

5.52 Where the agencies most involved judge that a child may continue to suffer, or to be at risk of suffering significant harm, the social services department should convene a child protection conference. The aim of the conference is to enable those professionals most involved with the child and family, and the family themselves, to assess all relevant information, and plan how to safeguard the child and promote his or her welfare.

The Initial Child Protection Conference

Purpose

5.53 The initial child protection conference brings together family members, the child where appropriate, and those professionals most involved with the child and family, following s.47 enquiries. Its purpose is:

- to bring together and analyse in an inter-agency setting the information which has been obtained about the child's health, development and functioning, and the parents' or carers' capacity to ensure the child's safety and promote the child's health and development;

- to make judgements about the likelihood of a child suffering significant harm in future; *and*

- to decide what future action is needed to safeguard the child and promote his or her welfare, how that action will be taken forward, and with what intended outcomes.

Timing

5.54 The timing of an initial child protection conference will depend on the urgency of the case and on the time needed to obtain relevant information about the child and family. If the conference is to reach well-informed decisions based on evidence, it should take place following adequate preparation and assessment. At the same time, cases where children are at risk of significant harm should not be allowed to drift. Consequently, all initial child protection conferences should take place within 15 working days of the strategy discussion.

Attendance

5.55 Those attending conferences should be there because they have a significant contribution to make, arising from professional expertise, knowledge of the child or family or both. There should be sufficient information and expertise available – through personal representation and written reports – to enable the conference to make an informed decision about what action is needed to safeguard the child and promote his or her welfare, and to make realistic and workable proposals for taking that action forward. At the same time, a conference which is larger than it needs to be can inhibit discussion and intimidate the child and family members. Those who have a relevant contribution to make may include:

- family members (including the wider family);

- social services staff who have undertaken an assessment of the child and family;

- foster carers (current or former);

- professionals involved with the child (e.g. health visitors, midwife, school nurse, *guardian ad litem*, paediatrician, education staff, early years staff, the GP);

- professionals involved with the parents (e.g. family support services, adult mental health services, probation, the GP);

- those involved in enquiries (e.g. the police);

- local authority legal services (child care);

- NSPCC or other involved voluntary organisations;

- a representative of the armed services, in cases where there is a Service connection.

5.56 The relevant ACPC protocol should specify a required quorum for attendance, and list those who should be invited to attend, provided that they have a relevant contribution to make. As a minimum, at every conference there should be attendance by social services and at least two other professional groups or agencies, who have had direct contact with the child who is the subject of the conference. In addition, attendees may also include those whose contribution relates to their professional expertise or responsibility for relevant services. In exceptional cases, where a child has not had relevant contact with three agencies (i.e. the SSD and two others), this minimum quorum may be breached. Professionals and agencies who are invited but are unable to attend should submit a written report.

Involving the Child and Family Members

5.57 Before a conference is held, the purpose of a conference, who will attend, and the way in which it will operate, should always be explained to a child of sufficient age and understanding, and to the parents and involved family members. The parents should normally be invited to attend the conference and helped fully to participate. Social services should give parents information about local advice and advocacy agencies, and explain that they may bring an advocate, friend or supporter. The child, subject to consideration about age and understanding, should be given the opportunity to attend if s/he wishes, and to bring an advocate, friend or supporter. Where the child's attendance is neither desired by him/her nor appropriate, the social services professional who is working most closely with the child should ascertain what his/her wishes and feelings are, and make these known to the conference.

5.58 The involvement of family members should be planned carefully. It may not always be possible to involve all family members at all times in the conference, for example, if one parent is the alleged abuser or if there is a high level of conflict between family members. Adults and any children who wish to make representations to the conference may not wish to speak in front of one another. Exceptionally, it may be necessary to exclude one or more family members from a conference, in whole or in part. The conference is primarily about the child, and while the presence of the family is normally welcome, those professionals attending must be able to share information in a safe and non-threatening environment. Professionals may themselves have concerns about violence or intimidation, which should be communicated in advance to the conference chair. ACPC procedures should set out criteria for excluding a parent or carer, including the evidence required. A strong risk of violence or intimidation by a family member at or subsequent to the conference, towards a child or anybody else, might be one reason for exclusion. The possibility that a parent/carer may be prosecuted for an offence against a child is not in itself a reason for exclusion although in these circumstances the chair should take advice from the police about any implications arising from an alleged perpetrator's attendance. If criminal proceedings have been instigated, the view of the Crown Prosecution Service should be taken into account. The decision to exclude a parent or carer from the child protection conference rests with the chair of the conference, acting within ACPC procedures. If the parents are excluded, or are unable or unwilling to attend a child protection conference, they should be enabled to communicate their views to the conference by another means.

Chairing the Conference

5.59 A professional who is independent of operational or line management responsibilities for the case should chair the conference. The status of the chair should be sufficient to ensure inter-agency commitment to the conference and the child protection plan. Wherever possible, the same person should also chair subsequent child protection reviews in respect of a specific child. The responsibilities of the chair include:

- meeting the child and family members in advance, to ensure that they understand the purpose of the conference and what will happen;

- setting out the purpose of the conference to all present, determining the agenda and emphasising the confidential nature of the occasion;

- enabling all those present, and absent contributors, to make their full contribution to discussion and decision-making; *and*

- ensuring that the conference takes the decisions required of it, in an informed, systematic and explicit way.

5.60 A conference chair should be trained in the role and should have:

- a good understanding and professional knowledge of children's welfare and development, and best practice in working with children and families;

- the ability to look objectively at, and assess the implications of the evidence on which judgements should be based;

- skills in chairing meetings in a way which encourages constructive participation, while maintaining a clear focus on the welfare of the child and the decisions which need to be taken; *and*

- knowledge and understanding of anti-discriminatory practice.

Information for the Conference

5.61 Social services should provide to the conference a written report which summarises and analyses the information obtained in the course of the initial assessment and s.47 enquiries, guided by the framework set out in the *Framework for the Assessment of Children in Need and their Families*. It is, of course, unlikely that a core assessment will have been completed in time for the conference, given the 35 working day period that such assessments are expected to require. The report should include:

- a chronology of significant events and agency and professional contact with the child and family;

- information on the child's current and past state of health and development;

- information on the capacity of the parents and other family members to ensure the child's safety from harm, and to promote the child's health and development;

- the expressed views, wishes and feelings of the child, parents, and other family members; *and*

- analysis of the implications of the information obtained for the child's future safety, health and development.

Parents and children, where relevant, should be provided with a copy of this report in advance of the conference which should also be explained and discussed in advance of the conference itself, in the preferred language(s) of the family.

5.62 Other professionals attending the conference should bring with them details of their involvement with the child and family, and information concerning their knowledge of the child's health and development, and the capacity of the parents to safeguard the child and promote the child's health and development. It is good practice for contributors to provide in advance a written report to the conference which should be made available to those attending. Children and family members should be helped in advance to think about what they want to convey to the conference and how best to get their points across on the day. Some may find it helpful to provide their own written report, which they may be assisted to prepare by their adviser/advocate.

5.63 All those providing information should take care to distinguish between fact, observation, allegation and opinion.

5.64 The conference should consider the following question when determining whether to register a child:

- **Is the child at continuing risk of significant harm?**

The test should be that either:

- the child can be shown to have suffered ill-treatment or impairment of health or development as a result of physical, emotional, or sexual abuse or neglect, and professional judgement is that further ill-treatment or impairment are likely; *or*

- professional judgement, substantiated by the findings of enquiries in this individual case or by research evidence, is that the child is likely to suffer ill-treatment or the impairment of health or development as a result of physical, emotional, or sexual abuse or neglect;

If the child is at continuing risk of significant harm, it will therefore be the case that safeguarding the child requires inter-agency help and intervention delivered through a formal child protection plan. It is also the role of the initial child protection conference to formulate the outline child protection plan, in as much detail as is possible.

5.65 Conference participants should base their judgements on all the available evidence obtained through existing records, the initial assessment and the fuller s.47 enquiries. The method of reaching a decision within the conference on whether the test for registration is satisfied, should be set out in the relevant ACPC protocol. The decision-making process should be based on the views of all agencies represented at the conference, and also take into account any written contributions that have been made.

5.66 If a decision is taken that the child is at continuing risk of significant harm and hence in need of a child protection plan and registration, the chair should determine under which category of abuse the child's name should be registered. The category used in registration (i.e. physical, emotional, sexual abuse or neglect) will indicate to those consulting the register the primary presenting concerns at the time of registration.

5.67 A child's name may not be placed on the register, but he or she may nonetheless be in need of help to promote his or her health or development. In these circumstances, the conference should ensure that arrangements are in place to consider with the family what further help and support might be offered. Subject to the family's views and consent, it may be appropriate to continue with a core assessment of the child's needs to help determine what support might best help promote the child's health and development. Where the child's needs are complex, inter-agency working will continue to be important.

5.68 Where a child's name is placed on the register, the act of registration itself confers no protection on a child, and should always be accompanied by a child protection plan. It is the responsibility of the conference to consider and make recommendations on how agencies, professionals and the family should work together to ensure that the child will be safeguarded from harm in the future. This should enable both professionals and the family to understand exactly what is expected of them and what they can expect of others. Specific tasks include the following:

- appointing a key worker;

- identifying the membership of a core group of professionals and family members who will develop and implement the child protection plan as a detailed working tool;

- establishing how children, parents (including all those with parental responsibility) and wider family members should be involved in the planning and implementation process, and the support, advice and advocacy available to them;

- establishing timescales for meetings of the core group, production of a child protection plan, and for child protection review meetings;

- identifying in outline what further core and specialist assessments of the child and family are required to make sound judgements on how best to safeguard the child and promote his or her welfare;

- outlining the child protection plan, especially, identifying what needs to change in order to safeguard the child;

- considering the need for a contingency plan if circumstances change quickly; *and*

- clarifying the different purpose and remit of the initial conference, the core group, and the child protection review conference.

5.69 The outline child protection plan should:

- identify risks of significant harm to the child and ways in which the child can be protected through an inter-agency plan based on assessment findings;

- establish short-term and longer-term aims and objectives that are clearly linked to reducing the risk of harm to the child and promoting the child's welfare;

- be clear about who will have responsibility for what actions – including actions by family members – within what specified timescales; *and*

- outline ways of monitoring and evaluating progress against the plan.

5.70 The conference should agree a date for the first child protection review conference, and under what circumstances it might be necessary to convene the conference before that date.

Complaints About a Child Protection Conference

5.71 Parents/carers and, on occasion children, may have concerns about which they may wish to make representations or complain, in respect of one or more of the following aspects of the functioning of child protection conferences:

- the process of the conference;

- the outcome, in terms of the fact of and/or the category of initial or continuing registration;

- a decision not to register or to de-register.

Complaints about individual agencies, their performance and provision (or non-provision) of services should be responded to in accordance with the relevant agency's complaints handling process. For example, Social Services Departments are required (by s.26 of the Children Act 1989) to establish complaints procedures to deal with complaints arising in respect of Part III of the Act.

5.72 Complaints about aspects of the functioning of conferences described above should be addressed to the conference chair. Such complaints should be passed on to the social service department which, since they relate to Part V of the Children Act 1989, should be responded to in accordance with the Complaints Directions 1990[5]. In considering and responding to complaints, the local authority should form an inter-agency panel made up of senior representatives from ACPC member agencies. The panel should consider whether the relevant inter-agency protocols and procedures have been observed correctly, and whether the decision that is being complained about follows reasonably from the proper observation of the protocol(s).

5.73 In addition, representations and complaints may be received by individual agencies in

---

5. The Directions are based on s.7B of the Local Authority Social Services Act 1970, inserted by s.50 of the National Health Service and Community Care Act 1990.

respect of services provided (or not provided) as a consequence of assessments and conferences, including those set out in child protection plans. Such concerns should be responded to by the relevant agency in accordance with its own processes for responding to such matters.

Administrative Arrangements and Record Keeping

5.74 Those attending should be notified of conferences as far in advance as possible, and the conference held at a time and place likely to be convenient to as many people as possible. All child protection conferences, both initial and review, should have a dedicated person to take notes and produce minutes of the meeting. The written record of the conference is a crucial working document for all relevant professionals and the family. It should include the essential facts of the case; a summary of discussion at the conference, which accurately reflects contributions made; all decisions reached, with information outlining the reasons for decisions; and a translation of decisions into an outline or revised child protection plan enabling, everyone to be clear about their tasks. A copy should be sent as soon as possible after the conference to all those who attended or were invited to attend, including family members, except for any part of the conference from which they were excluded. The record is confidential and should not be passed by professionals to third parties without the consent of either the conference chair or the key worker. However, in cases of criminal proceedings, the police may reveal the existence of the notes to the CPS in accordance with the Criminal Procedure and Investigation Act 1996. Child protection conference minutes, and other records associated with the registration process, should be retained by the recipient agencies and professionals in accordance with their record retention policies.

Action Following the Initial Child Protection Conference

The Role of the Key Worker

5.75 When a conference decides that a child's name should be placed on the child protection register, one of the child care agencies with statutory powers (the social services department or the NSPCC) should carry future child care responsibility for the case and designate a member of its social work staff to be the key worker. Each child placed on the child protection register should have a named key worker.

5.76 The key worker is responsible for making sure that the outline child protection plan is developed into a more detailed inter-agency plan. S/he should complete the core assessment of the child and family, securing contributions from Core Group members and others as necessary. The key worker is also responsible for acting as lead worker for the inter-agency work with the child and family. S/he should co-ordinate the contribution of family members and other agencies to planning the actions which need to be taken, putting the child protection plan into effect, and reviewing progress against the objectives set out in the plan. It is important that the role of the key worker is fully explained at the initial child protection conference and at the core group.

The Core Group

5.77 The core group is responsible for developing the child protection plan as a detailed working tool, and implementing it, within the outline plan agreed at the initial child protection conference. Membership should include the key worker, who leads the core group, the child if appropriate, family members, and professionals or foster carers who will have direct contact with the family. Although the key worker has the lead role, all members of the core group are jointly responsible for the formulation and implementation of the child protection plan, refining the plan as needed, and monitoring progress against specified objectives in the plan.

5.78 Core groups are an important forum for working with parents, wider family members, and children of sufficient age and understanding. It can often be difficult for parents to agree to a child protection plan within the confines of a formal conference. Their agreement may be forged later when details of the plan are worked out in the core group. Sometimes there may be conflicts of interest between family members who have a relevant interest in the work of the core group. The child's best interests should always have precedence over the interests of other family members.

5.79 The first meeting of the core group should take place within 10 working days of the initial child protection conference. The purpose of this first meeting is to flesh out the child protection plan and decide what steps need to be taken by whom to complete the core assessment on time. Thereafter, core groups should meet sufficiently regularly to facilitate working together, monitor actions and outcomes against the child protection plan, and make any necessary changes as circumstances change.

5.80 There should be a written note recording action agreed at core group meetings and decisions taken.

The Child Protection Plan

5.81 The initial child protection conference is responsible for agreeing an outline child protection plan. Professionals and parents/carers should develop the details of the plan in the core group. The aim of the plan is to:

* safeguard the child from further harm;

* promote the child's health and development; *and*

* provided it is in the best interests of the child, to support the family and wider family members to promote the welfare of their child.

5.82 The child protection plan should set out what work needs to be done, why, when and by whom. The plan should:

* describe the identified needs of the child, and what therapeutic services are required;

* include specific, achievable, child-focused objectives intended to safeguard the child and promote his or her welfare;

* include realistic strategies and specific actions to achieve the objectives;

* clearly identify roles and responsibilities of professionals and family members, including the nature and frequency of contact by professionals with children and family members;

* lay down points at which progress will be reviewed, and the means by which progress will be judged; *and*

* set out clearly the roles and responsibilities of those professionals with routine contact with the child, e.g. health visitors, GPs and teachers, as well as any specialist or targeted support to the child and family.

5.83 The child protection plan should take into consideration the wishes and feelings of the child, and the views of the parents, insofar as this is consistent with the child's welfare. The key worker should make every effort to ensure that the children and parents have a clear understanding of the objectives of the plan, that they accept it and are willing to work to it. The plan should be constructed with the family in their first language and they should receive a written copy in their first language. If family members' preferences are not accepted about how best to safeguard the child, the reasons for this should be explained. Families should be told about their right to complain and make representations, and how to do so.

5.84 All members of the core group have equal ownership of and responsibility for the child protection plan, and should co-operate to achieve its aims.

Assessment

5.85 Within 42 working days of beginning the initial assessment, the social services department should have completed a core assessment in respect of every child who has been placed on the child protection register. Where a child is not registered but meets the criteria for a core assessment as a 'child in need' then – provided that the parents wish an assessment to take place – this too should take place within the same timescale. For those children who are the subject of a child protection plan, the core assessment should be carried out in accordance with the recommendations of the initial child protection conference, as developed by the core group, and should be consistent with guidance in the Framework for the Assessment of Children in Need and their Families. It should build on information obtained in the course of initial assessment and the fuller s.47 enquiries.

5.86 Completion of the core assessment, for all children 'in need', should include an analysis of the child's developmental needs and the parents' capacity to respond to those needs, including parents' capacity to ensure that the child is safe from harm. It may be necessary to commission specialist assessments (e.g. from child and adolescent mental health services) which it may not be possible to complete within the 42 day period. This should not delay the drawing together of the core assessment findings at this point.

5.87 The analysis of the child's needs should provide evidence on which to base judgements and plans on how best to safeguard a child, promote his or her welfare, and support parents in promoting their children's welfare. In respect of those children on the child protection register, this analysis of the child's needs should underpin the child protection plan.

The Written Agreement

5.88 Parents should be clear about the causes of concern which resulted in the child's name being placed on the child protection register, what needs to change, and about what is expected of them as part of the plan for safeguarding the child. All parties should be clear about the respective roles and responsibilities of family members and different agencies in implementing the plan. It is good practice to produce a written agreement as part of, or additional to the plan, which is negotiated between the child, the family and professionals regarding the implementation of the plan.

Intervention

5.89 Decisions about how to intervene, including what services to offer, should be based on evidence about what is likely to work best to bring about good outcomes for the child. A number of aspects of intervention should be considered in the context of the child protection plan, in the light of evidence from assessment on the child's health and development needs, the parents' capacity to respond appropriately to the child's needs, and the wider family circumstances. Intervention may have a number of inter-related components:

- action to make a child safe;
- action to help promote a child's health and development;

- action to help a parent/carer in safeguarding a child and promoting his or her welfare;

- therapy for an abused child; *and*

- support or therapy for a perpetrator of abuse.

The Child Protection Review Conference

Timescale

5.90 The first child protection review conference should be held within three months of the initial child protection conference, and further reviews should be held at intervals of not more than six months for as long as the child's name remains on the child protection register. This is to ensure that momentum is maintained in the process of safeguarding the registered child. Attendees should include those most involved with the child and family in the same way as at an initial child protection conference, and the ACPC protocols for establishing a quorum should apply.

Purpose

5.91 The purpose of the child protection review is to review the safety, health and development of the child against intended outcomes set out in the child protection plan; to ensure that the child continues adequately to be safeguarded; and to consider whether the child protection plan should continue in place or should be changed. The review requires as much preparation, commitment and management as the initial child protection conference. Every review should consider explicitly whether the child continues to be at risk of significant harm, and hence continues to need safeguarding through adherence to a formal child protection plan. If not, then the child's name may be removed from the child protection register. The same ACPC decision-making procedure should be used to reach a judgement on de-registration as is used at the initial child protection conference in respect of registration. As with initial child protection conferences, the relevant ACPC protocol should specify a required quorum for attendance at review conferences.

5.92 The core group has a collective responsibility to produce reports for the child protection review which together provide an overview of work undertaken by family members and professionals, and evaluate the impact on the child's welfare against the objectives set out in the child protection plan.

De-Registration

5.93 A child's name may removed from the register if:

- it is judged that the child is no longer at continuing risk of significant harm requiring safeguarding by means of a child protection plan (e.g. the risk of harm has been reduced by action taken through the child protection plan; the child and family's circumstances have changed; or re-assessment of the child and family indicates that a child protection plan is not necessary). Under these circumstances, only a child protection review conference can decide that registration is no longer necessary;

- the child and family have moved permanently to another local authority area. In such cases, the receiving local authority should convene a child protection conference within 15 working days of being notified of the move, only after which event may de-registration take place in respect of the original local authority's child protection register;

- the child has reached 18 years of age, has died or has permanently left the UK.

5.94 When a child's name is removed from the register, notification should be sent, as minimum, to all those agencies representatives who were invited to attend the initial child protection conference which led to the registration.

5.95 A child whose name is removed from the register may still require additional support and services and de-registration should never lead to the automatic withdrawal of help. The key worker should discuss with the parents and the child what services might be wanted and needed, based upon the re-assessment of the child and family.

Children Looked After by the Local Authority

5.96 The Review of Children's Cases Regulations 1991 apply to local authorities that are looking after children; to voluntary organisations which accommodate children under Section 59 of the Children Act and registered children's homes which accommodated children not looked after by local authorities. The Review Regulations make clear provision for the frequency with which children's cases are to be reviewed by the responsible authority.

5.97 Where children looked after are also subject to a child protection review conference the overriding principle must be that the systems are integrated and carefully monitored in a way which promotes a child centred and not a bureaucratic approach. It is important to link the timing of a child protection review conference with the review under the Review Regulations to ensure that information from the former is brought to the review meeting, and informs the overall care planning process.

Pre-Birth Child Protection Conferences

5.98 Where s.47 enquiries give rise to concern that an unborn child may be at future risk of significant harm, the social services department may need to convene an initial child protection conference prior to the child's birth. Such a conference should have the same status, and proceed in the same way, as other initial child protection conferences, including decisions about registration. The involvement of midwifery services is vital in such cases.

The Child Protection Register

5.99 A central register should be maintained for each area covered by a social services department. The register should list all the children resident in the area (including those who have been placed there by another local authority or agency) who are considered to be at continuing risk of significant harm, and for whom there is a child protection plan.

5.100 The principal purpose of the register is to make agencies and professionals aware of those children who are judged to be at continuing risk of significant harm and in need of active safeguarding. Consequently, it is important that agencies and professionals who have concerns about a child are able to make enquiries of the register. It is essential that both police and health professionals have access to the register both in and outside office hours.

5.101 Children should be registered under one or more of the categories of physical, emotional, or sexual abuse or neglect, according to a decision by the chair of the child protection conference. The categories used for registration help indicate to those consulting the register the nature of presenting concerns. Recording information in this way also allows for the collation and analysis of information locally and nationally. The categories selected should reflect all the information obtained in the course of s.47

enquiries and subsequent analysis and should not just relate to one or more abusive incidents.

Managing the Child Protection Register

5.102 Child protection registers covering each local authority area should be managed within the social services department by an identified custodian, normally an experienced social worker from within the social services department. The register should be kept up-to-date and its contents should be confidential other than to legitimate enquirers. The register should be accessible at all times to such enquirers. The details of enquirers should always be checked before information is provided.

5.103 If an enquiry is made about a child and the name is on the register, the enquirer should be given the name of the child's key worker. If an enquiry is made about a child at the same address as a child on the register, the custodian should ensure that this information is passed on to the registered child's key worker. If an enquiry is made but the child's name is not on the register, this should be recorded together with the advice given to the enquirer. In the event of there being a second enquiry about a non-registered child, not only should the fact of the earlier enquiry be notified to the later enquirer, but the custodian should also refer the child to the social services department as a child who may be in need.

5.104 The Department of Health holds lists of custodians of child protection registers and should be notified of any changes in custodians.

6

Child protection in specific circumstances

Introduction

6.1   This chapter outlines some special considerations that apply to safeguarding children in a range of specific circumstances. It adds to, rather than substitutes for Chapter 5, which sets out the basic framework of action to be taken in all circumstances when a parent, professional, or any other person has concerns about the welfare of a child.

Children Living Away From Home

General

6.2   Revelations of the widespread abuse and neglect of children living away from home have done much to raise awareness of the particular vulnerability of children in a residential setting. Many of these have focused on sexual abuse, but physical and emotional abuse and neglect – including peer abuse, bullying and substance misuse – are equally a threat in institutional settings. There should never be complacency that these are problems of the past – there is a need for continuing vigilance.

6.3   Concern for the safety of children living away from home has to be put in the context of attention to the overall developmental needs of such children, and a concern for the best possible outcomes for their health and development. Every setting in which children live away from home should provide the same basic safeguards against abuse, founded on an approach which promotes their general welfare and protects them from harm of all kinds, and treats them with dignity and respect.

6.4   ACPC procedures should include a clear policy statement that local child protection procedures apply in every situation, including children living away from home. Individual agencies should have clear and unambiguous procedures in line with the ACPC's arrangements.

Basic Safeguards

6.5   There are a number of essential safeguards which should be observed in all settings in which children live away from home, including foster care, residential care, private fostering, health settings, residential schools, prisons, young offenders institutions and secure units. Where services are not directly provided, basic safeguards should be explicitly addressed in contracts with external providers. These safeguards include that:

- children feel valued and respected and their self-esteem is promoted;
- there is an openness on the part of the institution to the external world and external scrutiny, including openness with families and the wider community;
- staff and foster carers are trained in all aspects of safeguarding children; alert to

children's vulnerabilities and risks of harm; and knowledgeable about how to implement child protection procedures;

* children have ready access to a trusted adult outside the institution, e.g. a family member, the child's social worker, independent visitor, children's advocate. Children should be made aware of the help they could receive from independent advocacy services, external mentors, and ChildLine;

* complaints procedures are clear, effective, user friendly and are readily accessible to children and young people, including those with disabilities and those for whom English is not a first language. Procedures should address informal as well as formal complaints. Systems that do not promote open communication about 'minor' complaints will not be responsive to major ones, and a pattern of 'minor' complaints may indicate more deeply seated problems in management and culture which need to be addressed. There should be a complaints register in every children's home which records all representations or complaints, the action taken to address them, and the outcomes;

* recruitment and selection procedures are rigorous and create a high threshold of entry to deter abusers (see Chapter 7);

* clear procedures and support systems are in place for dealing with expressions of concern by staff and carers about other staff or carers. Organisations should have a code of conduct instructing staff on their duty to their employer and their professional obligation to raise legitimate concerns about the conduct of colleagues or managers. There should be a guarantee that procedures can be invoked in ways which do not prejudice the 'whistle-blower's' own position and prospects;

* there is respect for diversity and sensitivity to race, culture, religion, gender, sexuality and disability;

* there is effective supervision and support, which extends to temporary staff and volunteers; *and*

* staff and carers are alert to the risks to children in the external environment from people prepared to exploit the additional vulnerability of children living away from home.

Peer Abuse

6.6   Children, particularly those living away from home, are also vulnerable to abuse by their peers. Such abuse should always be taken as seriously as abuse perpetrated by an adult. It should be subject to the same child protection procedures as apply in respect of any child who is suffering, or at risk of suffering significant harm from an adverse source. A significant proportion of sex offences are committed by teenagers and, on occasion, by younger children. Staff in a residential setting need clear guidance and training to identify the difference between consenting and abusive, appropriate or exploitative peer relationships. Staff should not dismiss some abusive sexual behaviour as 'normal' between young people and should not develop high thresholds before taking action (see also paras. 6.31–6.37).

Race and Racism

6.7   Children from black and minority ethnic groups (and their parents) are likely to have experienced harassment, racial discrimination and institutional racism. Although racism causes significant harm it is not, in itself, a category of abuse. The experience of racism is likely to affect the responses of the child and family to assessment and enquiry processes. Failure to consider the effects of racism will undermine efforts to protect children from other forms of significant harm. The effects of racism differ for different communities and individuals, and should not be assumed to be uniform. The specific needs of children of mixed parentage and refugee children should be given attention. In particular, the need for neutral, high quality, gender-appropriate translation or interpretation services should be taken into account when working with children and families whose language of normal use is not English. All organisations working with children, including those operating in areas where black and minority ethnic communities are numerically small, should address institutional racism, defined in the Macpherson Inquiry Report on Stephen Lawrence as "the collective failure by an organisation to provide an appropriate and professional service to people on account of their race, culture and/or religion".

Bullying

6.8 Bullying may be defined as deliberately hurtful behaviour, usually repeated over a period of time, where it is difficult for those bullied to defend themselves. It can take many forms, but the three main types are physical (e.g. hitting, kicking, theft), verbal (e.g. racist or homophobic remarks, threats, name calling) and emotional (e.g. isolating an individual from the activities and social acceptance of their peer group). The damage inflicted by bullying can frequently be underestimated. It can cause considerable distress to children, to the extent that it affects their health and development or, at the extreme, causes them significant harm (including self-harm). All settings in which children are provided with services or are living away from home should have in place rigorously enforced anti-bullying strategies.

Foster Care

6.9 Foster care is undertaken in the private domain of carers' own homes. This may make it more difficult to identify abusive situations and for children to find a voice outside the family. Social workers are required to see children in foster care on their own for a proportion of visits, and evidence of this should be recorded.

6.10 Foster carers should monitor the whereabouts of their foster children, their patterns of absence and contacts. Foster carers should notify the placing authority of any unauthorised absence by a child.

6.11 Social services' duty to conduct s.47 enquiries, when there are concerns about significant harm to a child, applies on the same basis to children in foster care as it does to children in their own families. Enquiries should consider the safety of any other children living in the household, including the foster carers' own children.

6.12 Where foster carers care for children who have been abused, who may have been abused or who may have abused others, they have a right to be given full information, both in the interests of the child and of the foster family.

Allegations of Abuse Made Against a Professional, Foster Carer, or Volunteer

General

6.13 Experience has shown that children can be subjected to abuse by those who work with them in any and every setting. All allegations of abuse of children by a professional, staff member, foster carer or volunteer (from ACPC member agencies) should therefore be taken seriously and treated in accordance with local child protection procedures. Other organisations which provide services for children (including day care, leisure, churches, other places of worship and voluntary services) should have a procedure for handling such allegations which is consistent with this guidance and with ACPC procedures. There should be clear written procedures in place which are available for scrutiny by service users, and which are supported by the training and supervision of staff. It is essential that all allegations are examined objectively by staff who are independent of the service, organisation or institution concerned.

Investigating Allegations

6.14 Where allegations of abuse are made against a staff member or volunteer, whether contemporary in nature, historical, or both, the matter should be referred to the social services department, in the same way as any other concern about possible abuse. Social services should always discuss the case with the police at the first opportunity if a criminal offence may have been committed against a child. Investigations into allegations relating to a member of social services' own staff (or foster carers) should involve an independent person, from outside the relevant service or institution or from outside the authority, e.g. another local authority or NSPCC.

6.15 In recent years, there have been a number of widely reported cases of historical abuse, usually of an organised or multiple nature (see para. 6.24). Such cases have generally come to light after adults have reported abuse that they had experienced when children, while living away from home in settings provided by local authorities, the voluntary sector or independent providers. When such allegations are made, they should be responded to in the same way as contemporary concerns, in terms of prompt referral to the relevant social services department, and discussion with the police if it appears that a criminal offence has been committed.

6.16 Any investigation may well have three related, but independent strands:

- child protection enquiries, relating to the safety and welfare of any children who are or who may have been involved;

- a police investigation into a possible offence;

- disciplinary procedures, where it appears that the allegations may amount to misconduct or gross misconduct on the part of staff. A similar, if simpler, process will need to be in place for responding to concerns about volunteers.

6.17 It is essential that the common facts of the alleged abuse are applied independently to each of the three strands of possible enquiries/investigation. The fact that a prosecution is not possible does not mean that action in relation to safeguarding children, or employee discipline, is not necessary or feasible. The important thing is that each aspect is thoroughly assessed, and a definite conclusion reached.

6.18 The risk of harm to children posed by the person under investigation should be effectively evaluated and managed – in respect of the child(ren) involved in the allegations, and any other children in the individual's home, work or community life.

6.19 Staff, foster carers, volunteers and other individuals about whom there are concerns should be treated fairly and honestly, and should be provided with support throughout the investigation process as should others who are also involved. They should be helped to understand the concerns expressed and the processes being operated, and be clearly informed of the outcome of any investigation and the implications for disciplinary or related processes. The investigation should be completed as quickly as possible consistent with its effective conduct. The police and other relevant agencies should always agree jointly when to inform the suspect of allegations which are the subject of criminal proceedings.

6.20 Parents of affected children should be given information about the concerns, advised on the processes to be followed, and the outcomes reached. The provision of information and advice must take place in a manner that does not impede the proper exercise of enquiry, disciplinary and investigative processes.

6.21 Those undertaking investigations should be alert to any sign or pattern which suggests that the abuse is more widespread or organised than it appears at first sight, or that it involves other perpetrators or institutions. It is important not to assume that initial signs will necessarily be related directly to abuse, and to consider occasions where boundaries have been blurred, inappropriate behaviour has taken place, and matters such as fraud, deception or pornography have been involved.

6.22 If an allegation is substantiated, the managers or commissioners of the service should think widely about the lessons of the case and how they should be acted upon. This should include whether there are features of the organisation which may have contributed to the abuse occurring, or failed to prevent the abuse occurring. In some circumstances, a full case review may be appropriate (see Chapter 8).

The Protection of Children Act 1999

6.23 The Protection of Children Act 1999, when implemented, will require child care organisations (within the meaning of the Act) to refer the names of individuals considered unsuitable to work with children, to a Department of Health list, along with List 99 maintained by the Department for Education and Employment. It will also require child care organisations not to offer work to anyone so listed for any posts involving regular contact with children in a childcare capacity. It will provide for rights of appeal to an independent tribunal against inclusion on either list. Further details of the Act are at Appendix 3.

Investigating Organised or Multiple Abuse

6.24 Organised or multiple abuse may be defined as abuse involving one or more abuser and a number of related or non-related abused children and young people. The abusers concerned may be acting in concert to abuse children, sometimes acting in isolation, or may be using an institutional framework or position of authority to recruit children for abuse.

6.25 Organised and multiple abuse occur both as part of a network of abuse across a family or community, and within institutions such as residential homes or schools. Such abuse is profoundly traumatic for the children who become involved. Its investigation is time-consuming and demanding work requiring specialist skills from both police and social work staff. Some investigations become extremely complex because of the number of places and people involved, and the timescale over which abuse is alleged to have occurred. The complexity is heightened where, as in historical cases, the alleged victims are no longer living in the situations where the incidents occurred or where the alleged perpetrators are also no longer linked to the setting or employment role.

6.26 Each investigation of organised or multiple abuse will be different, according to the characteristics of each situation and the scale and complexity of the investigation. Each requires thorough planning, good inter-agency working, and attention to the welfare needs of the children involved. The guidance above on investigating allegations of abuse against professionals is equally relevant to investigating organised or multiple abuse within an institution. In addition, there are some important issues which should be addressed in all major investigations, and which should be reflected in local procedures:

* bring together a trusted and vetted team from police and social work (either social services or NSPCC or both) to manage and conduct major investigations where a

criminal investigation runs alongside child protection enquiries. Set out clearly the terms of engagement for the team. Emphasise the need for confidentiality. It is essential that the managers of the team have training and expertise in conducting investigations, legal processes, disciplinary proceedings, children's welfare; and profiles and methods of abusers (in cases of sexual abuse). Team members need expertise in conducting investigations, child protection processes, and children's welfare, and they should be committed to working closely together;

- involve the most senior managers from involved agencies at a strategic level. They should ensure that appropriate resources are deployed and staff are supported, and should agree upon the handling of political and media issues arising from the investigation;

- the police should appoint a Senior Investigating Officer of appropriate rank and experience, and should consider the use of Major Incident Room Standard Administrative Procedures and the Home Office Large Major Enquiry System;

- ensure that records are safely and securely stored;

- recognise and anticipate that an investigation may become more extensive than suggested by initial allegations;

- where a social services department's own staff (or foster carers) are being investigated, it is essential to ensure independence and objectivity on the part of the social work team. Where it is practicable, in the circumstances, to conduct a rigorous and impartial investigation using the authority's own staff, it is essential to ensure sufficient distance (in structural and geographical terms) between such staff and those being investigated. This means that the inclusion of staff members or managers from the institution or workplace under investigation should be considered with particular care;

- begin every investigation with a strategy discussion to agree terms of reference and ways of working. Relevant areas for decision-making include the timing, parameters and conduct of the investigation; lines of accountability and communication; the safe and secure storage of records; the deployment of staff and resources; and a communications strategy encompassing authority members, staff, children and families, the media, and SSI Social Care Region. Terms of reference should include assurances that the team will have full access to records and individuals who hold important information;

- secure access to expert legal advice. The inter-relationship between criminal, civil and employment processes is complex;

- use regular strategic planning meetings and reviews to consider the conduct of the investigation, next steps, and the effectiveness of joint working. Always minute meetings;

- agree clear written protocols between police, social services and other agencies in relation to all key operational and policy matters, including information sharing;

- consider first whether there are any children involved who need active safeguarding and/or therapeutic help, and how this should be achieved in a way which is consistent with the conduct of criminal investigations;

- make a thorough assessment of victims' needs, and provide services to meet those needs;

- it is good practice to provide a confidential and independent counselling service for victims and families. Agree guidelines with counselling and welfare services on disclosure of information, to avoid the contamination of evidence;

- provide care and support for the investigation team – much of the work may be difficult and distressing;

- put in place a means of identifying and acting on lessons learned from the investigation (e.g. in respect of policies, procedures and working practices which may have contributed to the abuse occurring) as the investigation proceeds, and at its close; *and*

- at the close of the investigation, assess its handling and identify lessons for conducting similar investigations in future.

Abuse of Disabled Children

6.27　The available UK evidence on the extent of abuse among disabled children suggests that disabled children are at increased risk of abuse, and that the presence of multiple disabilities appears to increase the risk of both abuse and neglect. Disabled children may be especially vulnerable to abuse for a number of reasons. Some disabled children may:

- have fewer outside contacts than other children;

- receive intimate personal care, possibly from a number of carers, which may both increase the risk of exposure to abusive behaviour, and make it more difficult to set and maintain physical boundaries;

- have an impaired capacity to resist or avoid abuse;

- have communication difficulties which may make it difficult to tell others what is happening;

- be inhibited about complaining because of a fear of losing services;

- be especially vulnerable to bullying and intimidation; *and/or*

- be more vulnerable than other children to abuse by their peers.

6.28　Safeguards for disabled children are essentially the same as for non-disabled children. There should be particular attention paid to promoting a high level of awareness of the risks and high standards of practice, and to strengthen the capacity of children and families to help themselves. Measures include:

- making it common practice to help disabled children make their wishes and feelings known in respect of their care and treatment;

- ensuring that disabled children receive appropriate personal, health, and social education (including sex education);

- making sure that all disabled children know how to raise concerns if they are worried or angry about something, and giving them access to a range of adults with whom they can communicate. Those disabled children with communication difficulties should have available to them at all times a means of being heard;

- an explicit commitment to, and understanding of all children's safety and welfare among providers of services used by disabled children;

- close contact with families, and a culture of openness on the part of services; *and*

- guidelines and training for staff on good practice in intimate care; working with children of the opposite sex; handling difficult behaviour; consent to treatment; anti-bullying strategies; and sexuality and sexual behaviour among young people living away from home.

6.29　Where there are concerns about the welfare of a disabled child, they should be acted upon in accordance with the guidance in Chapter 5, in the same way as with any other child. The same thresholds for action apply. It would be unacceptable if poor standards of care were tolerated for disabled children which would not be tolerated for non-disabled children. Where a disabled child has communication difficulties or learning difficulties, special attention should be paid to communication needs, and to ascertain the child's perception of events, and his or her wishes and feelings. In every area, social services and the police should be aware of non-verbal communication systems, when they might be useful and how to access them, and should know how to contact suitable interpreters or facilitators. Agencies should not make assumptions about the inability of a disabled child to give credible evidence, or to withstand the rigours of the court process. Each child should be assessed carefully, and helped and supported to participate in the criminal justice process when this is in the child's best interest and the interests of justice.

6.30 ACPCs have an important role in safeguarding disabled children through:

- raising awareness among children, families and services;

- identifying and meeting inter-agency training needs, which encourage the 'pooling' of expertise between those with knowledge and skills in respect of disabilities, and those with knowledge and skills in respect of child protection;

- ensuring that local policies and procedures for safeguarding children meet the needs of disabled children.

Abuse by Children and Young People

6.31 Work with children and young people who abuse others – including those who sexually abuse/offend – should recognise that such children are likely to have considerable needs themselves, and also that they may pose a significant risk of harm to other children. Evidence suggests that children who abuse others may have suffered considerable disruption in their lives, been exposed to violence within the family, may have witnessed or been subject to physical or sexual abuse, have problems in their educational development, and may have committed other offences. Such children and young people are likely to be children in need, and some will in addition be suffering or at risk of significant harm, and may themselves be in need of protection.

6.32 Children and young people who abuse others should be held responsible for their abusive behaviour, whilst being identified and responded to in a way which meets their needs as well as protecting others. Work with adult abusers has shown that many of them began committing abusing acts during childhood or adolescence, and that significant numbers themselves have been subjected to abuse. Early intervention with children and young people who abuse others may, therefore, play an important part in protecting the public by preventing the continuation or escalation of abusive behaviour.

6.33 Three key principles should guide work with children and young people who abuse others:

- there should be a co-ordinated approach on the part of youth justice, child welfare, education (including educational psychology) and health (including child and adolescent mental health) agencies;

- the needs of children and young people who abuse others should be considered separately from the needs of their victims; *and*

- an assessment should be carried out in each case, appreciating that these children may have considerable unmet developmental needs, as well as specific needs arising from their behaviour.

6.34 ACPCs and Youth Offending Teams should ensure that there is a clear operational framework in place within which assessment, decision-making and case management take place. Neither child welfare nor criminal justice agencies should embark upon a course of action that has implications for the other without appropriate consultation.

6.35   In assessing a child or young person who abuses another, relevant considerations include:

- the nature and extent of the abusive behaviours. In respect of sexual abuse, there are sometimes perceived to be difficulties in distinguishing between normal childhood sexual development and experimentation and sexually inappropriate or aggressive behaviour. Expert professional judgement may be needed, within the context of knowledge about normal child sexuality;

- the context of the abusive behaviours;

- the child's development, and family and social circumstances;

- needs for services, specifically focusing on the child's harmful behaviour as well as other significant needs; *and*

- the risks to self and others, including other children in the household, extended family, school, peer group or wider social network.

This risk is likely to be present unless: the opportunity to further abuse is ended, the young person has acknowledged the abusive behaviour and accepted responsibility and there is agreement by the young abuser and his/her family to work with relevant agencies to address the problem.

6.36   Decisions for local agencies (including the Crown Prosecution Service where relevant), according to the responsibilities of each, include:

- the most appropriate course of action within the criminal justice system, if the child is above the age of criminal responsibility;

- whether the young abuser should be the subject of a child protection conference; *and*

- what plan of action should be put in place to address the needs of the young abuser, detailing the involvement of all relevant agencies.

6.37   A young abuser should be the subject of a child protection conference if he or she is considered personally to be at risk of continuing significant harm. Where there is no reason to hold a child protection conference, there may still be a need for a multi-agency approach if the young abuser's needs are complex. Issues regarding suitable educational and accommodation arrangements often require skilled and careful consideration.

Domestic Violence

6.38   As outlined in Chapter 2, children may suffer both directly and indirectly if they live in households where there is domestic violence. Domestic violence is likely to have a damaging effect on the health and development of children, and it will often be appropriate for such children to be regarded as children in need. Everyone working with women and children should be alert to the frequent inter-relationship between domestic violence and the abuse and neglect of children. Where there is evidence of domestic violence, the implications for any children in the household should be considered, including the possibility that the children may themselves be subject to violence or other harm. Conversely, where it is believed that a child is being abused, those involved with the child and family should be alert to the possibility of domestic violence within the family.

6.39   The police are often the first point of contact with families in which domestic violence takes place. When responding to incidents of violence, the police should find out whether there are any children living in the household. There should be arrangements in place between police and social services, to enable the police to find out whether any such children are on the Child Protection Register. The police are already required to determine whether any court orders or injunctions are in force in respect of members of the household. It is good practice for the police to notify the social services department when they have responded to an incident of domestic violence and it is known that a child is a member of the household. If the police have specific concerns about the safety or welfare of a child, they should make a referral to the social services department citing the basis for their concerns. It is also important that there is clarity about whether the family is aware that a referral is to be made. Any response by social services to such referrals should be discreet, in terms of making contact with women in ways will not further endanger them or their children. In extreme cases, a child may be in need of immediate protection.

6.40   Normally, one serious incident or several lesser incidents of domestic violence where there is a child in the household would indicate that the social services department should carry out an initial assessment of the child and family, including consulting existing records. Children who are experiencing domestic violence may benefit from a range of support and services, and some may need safeguarding from harm. Often, supporting a non-violent parent is likely to be the most effective way of promoting the child's welfare. The police and other agencies have defined powers in criminal and civil law which can be used to help those who are subject to domestic violence.

6.41   There is an extensive range of services for women and children delivered through refuge projects operated by Women's Aid and others. These have a vital role in contributing to an inter-agency approach in child protection cases where domestic violence is an issue. In responding to situations where domestic violence may be present, consideration include:

- asking direct questions about domestic violence;

- checking whether domestic violence has occurred whenever child abuse is suspected and considering the impact of this at all stages of assessment, enquiries and intervention;

- identifying those who are responsible for domestic violence in order that relevant criminal justice responses may be made;

- providing women with full information about their legal rights and the extent and limits of statutory duties and powers;

- assisting women and children to escape from violence by providing relevant practical and other assistance;

- supporting non-abusing parents in making safe choices for themselves and their children; *and*

- working separately with each parent where domestic violence prevents non-abusing parents from speaking freely and participating without fear of retribution.

6.42   Domestic Violence Forums have been set up in many areas, to raise awareness of domestic violence, to promote co-ordination between agencies in preventing and responding to violence, and to encourage the development of services for those who are subjected to violence or suffer its effects. Each Domestic Violence Forum and ACPC should have clearly defined links, which should include cross-membership and identifying and working together on areas of common interest. The Domestic Violence Forum and ACPC should jointly contribute – in the context of the children's services plan – to an assessment of the incidence of children caught up in domestic violence, their needs, the adequacy of local arrangements to meet those needs, and the implications for local services. Further information on domestic violence and its impact on children is included in the reading material listed at Appendix 6.

Children Involved in Prostitution

6.43 Children involved in prostitution and other forms of commercial sexual exploitation should be treated primarily as the victims of abuse, and their needs require careful assessment. They are likely to be in need of welfare services and – in many cases – protection under the Children Act 1989. The problem is often hidden from view. ACPCs should actively enquire into the extent to which there is a local problem, and should not assume that it is not a local issue.

6.44 The Home Office and Department of Health jointly published draft guidance in December 1998 on children involved in prostitution. The guidance promotes an approach whereby agencies should work together to:

- recognise the problem;

- treat the child primarily as a victim of abuse;

- safeguard the children involved and promote their welfare;

- provide children with strategies to leave prostitution; *and*

- investigate and prosecute those who coerce, exploit and abuse children.

6.45 The guidance states that local agencies should develop inter-agency protocols to guide action when there are concerns that a child is involved in prostitution, including guidance on sharing concerns about a child's safety. The protocols should be consistent with ACPC procedures for safeguarding children, with procedures for working with children in need, and with relevant aspects of youth offending protocols. The identification of a child involved in prostitution, or at risk of being drawn into prostitution, should always trigger the agreed local procedures to ensure the child's safety and welfare, and to enable the police to gather evidence about abusers and coercers. The strong links that have been identified between prostitution and substance misuse should be borne in mind in the development of protocols.

6.46 Children involved in prostitution may be difficult to reach, and under very strong pressure to remain in prostitution. They may be fearful of being involved with the police or social services, and may respond best initially to informal contact from health or voluntary sector outreach workers. Gaining the child's trust and confidence is vital if he or she is to be helped to be safe and well, and diverted from prostitution.

Child Pornography and the Internet

6.47 The Internet has now become a significant tool in the distribution of child pornography. Adults are now using the Internet to try to establish contact with children with a view to 'grooming' them for inappropriate or abusive relationships.

6.48 As part of their role in preventing abuse and neglect, ACPCs may wish to consider activities to raise awareness about the safe use of the Internet by children, for example, by distributing information through education staff to parents, in relation to both school and home-based use of computers by children.

6.49 When somebody is discovered to have placed child pornography on the Internet, or accessed child pornography, the police should normally consider whether that individual might also be involved in the active abuse of children. In particular, the individual's access to children should be established, within the family and employment contexts and in other settings (e.g. work with children as a volunteer). If there are particular concerns about one or more specific children, there may be a need to carry out s.47 enquiries in respect of those children.

Children and Families Who Go Missing

6.50 Local agencies and professionals should bear in mind when working with children and families where there are outstanding child protection concerns (including where the concerns are about an unborn child who may be at future risk of significant harm) that a series of missed appointments or abortive home visits may indicate that the family have suddenly and unexpectedly moved out of the area. Social services and the police should be informed immediately such concerns arise.

6.51 Particular consideration needs to be given to appropriate legal interventions, where it appears that a child, for whom there are outstanding child protection concerns, may be removed from the UK by his/her family in order to evade the involvement of agencies with safeguarding responsibilities.

Female Genital Mutilation

6.52 The Prohibition of Female Circumcision Act 1985 makes female circumcision, excision or infibulation (female genital mutilation (FGM)) an offence, except on specific physical and mental health grounds. Available medical evidence indicates that FGM causes harm to those who experience it. A local authority may exercise its powers under s.47 of the Children Act 1989 if it has reason to believe that a child is likely to be or has been the subject of FGM.

6.53 Local agencies should be alert to the possibility of female circumcision among the ethnic minority communities known to practice it. In local areas where there are communities or individuals who traditionally practice FGM, ACPC policy should focus on a preventive strategy involving community education.

7

Some key principles

Introduction

7.1   There are some common principles and ways of working which should underpin the practice of all agencies and professionals working to safeguard children and promote their welfare. This chapter sets out some of the most important of these.

Working in Partnership with Children and Families

The Importance of Partnership in Child Protection

7.2   Family members have a unique role and importance in the lives of children, who attach great value to their family relationships. Family members know more about their family than any professional could possibly know, and well-founded decisions about a child should draw upon this knowledge and understanding. Family members should normally have the right to know what is being said about them, and to contribute to important decisions about their lives and those of their children. Research findings brought together in *Child Protection: Messages from Research* endorse the importance of good relationships between professionals and families in helping to bring about the best possible outcomes for children.

What is meant by Partnership in Child Protection?

7.3   Where there are concerns about significant harm to a child, social services departments have a statutory duty to make enquiries and if necessary, statutory powers to intervene to safeguard the child and promote his or her welfare. Where there is compulsory intervention in family life in this way, parents should still be helped and encouraged to play as full a part as possible in decisions about their child. Children of sufficient age and understanding should be kept fully informed of processes involving them, should be consulted sensitively, and decisions about their future should take account of their views.

7.4   The Challenge of Partnership in Child Protection outlines 15 basic principles for working in partnership, which are reproduced below.

7.5   Partnership does not mean always agreeing with parents or other adult family members, or always seeking a way forward which is acceptable to them. The aim of child protection processes is to ensure the safety and welfare of a child, and the child's interests should always be paramount. Some parents may feel hurt and angry and refuse to co-operate with professionals. Not all parents will be able to safeguard their children, even with help and support. Especially in child sexual abuse cases, some may be vulnerable to manipulation by a perpetrator of abuse. A minority of parents are actively dangerous to their children, other family members, or professionals, and are unwilling

1. Treat all family members as you would wish to be treated, with dignity and respect.

2. Ensure that family members know that the child's safety and welfare must be given first priority, but that each of them has a right to a courteous, caring and professionally competent service.

3. Take care not to infringe privacy any more than is necessary to safeguard the welfare of the child.

4. Be clear with yourself and with family members about your power to intervene, and the purpose of your professional involvement at each stage.

5. Be aware of the effects on family members of the power you have as a professional, and the impact and implications of what you say and do.

6. Respect the confidentiality of family members and your observations about them, unless they give permission for information to be passed to others or it is essential to do so to protect the child.

7. Listen to the concerns of children and their families, and take care to learn about their understanding, fears and wishes before arriving at your own explanations and plans.

8. Learn about and consider children within their family relationships and communities, including their cultural and religious contexts, and their place within their own families.

9. Consider the strengths and potential of family members, as well as their weaknesses, problems and limitations.

10. Ensure children, families and other carers know their responsibilities and rights, including any right to services, and their right to refuse services, and any consequences of doing so.

11. Use plain, jargon-free language appropriate to the age and culture of each person. Explain unavoidable technical and professional terms.

12. Be open and honest about your concerns and responsibilities, plans and limitations, without being defensive.

13. Allow children and families time to take in and understand concerns and processes. A balance needs to be found between appropriate speed and the needs of people who may need extra time in which to communicate.

14. Take care to distinguish between personal feelings, values, prejudices and beliefs, and professional roles and responsibilities, and ensure that you have good supervision to check that you are doing so.

15. If a mistake or misinterpretation has been made, or you are unable to keep to an agreement, provide an explanation. Always acknowledge any distress experienced by adults and children and do all you can to keep it to a minimum.

and/or unable to change. Always maintain a clear focus on the child's safety and what is best for the child.

Working in Partnership

7.6   Those working together to safeguard children should agree a common understanding in each case, and at each stage of work, of how children and families will be involved in child protection processes, and what information is shared with them. There should be a presumption of openness, joint decision making, and a willingness to listen to families and capitalise on their strengths, but the overarching principle should always be to act is in the best interests of the child. Some information known to professionals should be treated confidentially and should not be shared in front of some children or some adult family members. Such information might include personal health information about particular family members, unless consent has been given, or information which, if disclosed, could compromise criminal investigations or proceedings.

7.7 Agencies and professionals should be honest and explicit with children and families about professional roles, responsibilities, powers and expectations, and about what is and is not negotiable.

7.8 Working relationships with families should develop according to individual circumstances. From the outset, professionals should assess if, when and how the involvement of different family members – both children and adults – can contribute to safeguarding and promoting the welfare of a particular child or group of children. This assessment may change over time as more information becomes available or as families feel supported by professionals. Professional supervision and peer group discussions are important in helping to explore knowledge and perceptions of families' strengths and weaknesses and the safety and welfare of the child within the family.

7.9 Family structures are increasingly complex. In addition to those adults who have daily care of a child, estranged parents (e.g. birth fathers), grandparents, or other family members may play a significant part in the child's life, and some may have parental responsibility even if they are not involved in day to day care. Some children may have been supported during family difficulties by adults from outside the family. Professionals should make sure that they pay attention to the views of all those who have something significant to contribute to decisions about the child's future. Children can provide valuable help in identifying adults they see as important supportive influences in their lives.

7.10 Occasions may arise where relationships between parents, or other family members, are not productive in terms of working to safeguard children and promote their development. In such instances, agencies should respond sympathetically to a request for a change of worker, provided that such a change can be identified as being in the interests of the child who is the focus of concern.

Involving Children

7.11 Children of sufficient age and understanding often have a clear perception of what needs to be done to ensure their safety and well-being. Listening to children and hearing their messages requires training and special skills, including the ability to win their trust and promote a sense of safety. Most children feel loyalty towards those who care for them, and have difficulty saying anything against them. Many do not wish to share confidences, or may not have the language or concepts to describe what has happened to them. Some may fear reprisals or their removal from home.

7.12 Children and young people need to understand the extent and nature of their involvement in decision-making and planning processes. They should be helped to understand how child protection processes work, how they can be involved, and that they can contribute to decisions about their future in accordance with their age and understanding. However, they should understand that ultimately, decisions will be taken in the light of all the available information contributed by themselves, professionals, their parents and other family members, and other significant adults.

Family Group Conferences

7.13 In recent years, Family Group Conferences (FGCs) have been developed in a number of areas as a positive option for planning services for children and their families. There is a growing body of research about the impact and outcomes of FGCs.

7.14 FGCs are a process through which family members, including those in the wider family, are enabled to meet together to find solutions to difficulties which they and a child or young person in their family are facing. FGCs are not just a one-off meeting. They are an approach to planning and decision-making which uses the skills and experience of the wider family, as well as professionals. The definition of who is in a family should come from the family itself. It includes parents and extended family, as well as friends, neighbours and community members if they are considered part of the child's 'family'.

7.15 FGCs may be appropriate in a number of contexts where there is a plan or decision to be made. FGCs do not replace or remove the need for child protection conferences, which should always be held when the relevant criteria are met (see para. 5.52). They may be valuable, for example:

- for children in need, in a range of circumstances where a plan is required for the child's future welfare;

- where s.47 enquiries do not substantiate referral concerns about significant harm but where there is a need for support and services;

- where s.47 enquiries progress to a child protection conference, the conference may agree that an FGC is an appropriate vehicle for the core group to use to develop the outline child protection plan into a fully worked-up plan.

7.16 It is essential that all parties are provided with clear and accurate information, which will make effective planning possible. The family is the primary planning group in the process. Family members need to be able to understand what the issues are from the perspective of the professionals. The family and involved professionals should be clear about:

- what are the professional findings from any core assessment of the child and family;

- what the family understand about their current situation;

- what decisions are required;

- what decisions have already been taken;

- what is the family's scope of decision-making, and whether there are any issues/decisions which are not negotiable; *and*

- what resources are or might be available to implement any plan.

Within this framework, agencies and professionals should agree to support the plan if it does not place the child at risk of significant harm, and if the resources requested can be provided.

7.17 Where there are plans to use FGCs in situations where there are child protection concerns, they should be developed and implemented under the auspices of the ACPC. This will involve all relevant agencies in their development and relate their use to other relevant child protection policies and procedures. Inter-agency training will be needed to build the relevant skills needed to work with children and families in this way, and to promote confidence in and develop a shared understanding of the process.

7.18 Further information about FGCs is included among the reading material listed at Appendix 6.

Support, Advice and Advocacy to Children and Families

7.19 However sensitively enquiries are handled, many families perceive unasked – for professional involvement in their lives as painful and intrusive, particularly if they feel that their care of their children is being called into question. This should always be acknowledged. Agencies and professionals can do a considerable amount to make child protection processes less stressful for families by adopting the principles set out above. Families will also feel better supported if it is clear that interventions in their lives, while firmly focused on the safety and welfare of the child, are concerned also with the wider needs of the child and family.

7.20 Children and families may be supported through their involvement in child protection processes by advice and advocacy services, and they should always be informed of those services which exist locally and nationally (such as those provided by the Family Rights Group).

7.21 Where children and families are involved as witnesses in criminal proceedings, the police, witness support services and other services provided by Victim Support, can do a great deal to explain the process, make it feel less daunting and ensure that children are prepared for and supported in the court process. Information about the Criminal Injuries Compensation Scheme should also be provided in relevant cases.

Communication and Information

7.22 The social services department has a responsibility to make sure children and adults have all the information they need to help them understand child protection processes. Information should be clear and accessible and available in the family's first language.

7.23 If a child and/or family member has specific communication needs, because of language or disability, it may be necessary to use the services of an interpreter or specialist worker, or to make use of other aids to communication. Particular care should be taken in choosing an interpreter, having regard to their language skills, their understanding of the issues under discussion, their commitment to confidentiality, and their position in the wider community. There can be difficulties in using family members or friends as interpreters and this should be avoided. Children should not be used as interpreters.

Race, Ethnicity and Culture

7.24 Children from all cultures are subject to abuse and neglect. All children have a right to grow up safe from harm. In order to make sensitive and informed professional judgements about a child's needs, and parents' capacity to respond to their child's needs, it is important that professionals are sensitive to differing family patterns and lifestyles and to child rearing patterns that vary across different racial, ethnic and cultural groups. Professionals should also be aware of the broader social factors that serve to discriminate against black and minority ethnic people. Working in a multi-racial and multi-cultural society requires professionals and organisations to be committed to equality in meeting the needs of all children and families, and to understand the effects of racial harassment, racial discrimination and institutional racism, as well as cultural misunderstanding or misinterpretation.

7.25 The assessment process should maintain a focus on the needs of the individual child. It should always include consideration of the way religious beliefs and cultural traditions in different racial, ethnic and cultural groups influence their values, attitudes and behaviour, and the way in which family and community life is structured and organised. Cultural factors neither explain nor condone acts of omission or commission which place a child at risk of significant harm. Professionals should be aware of and work with the strengths and support systems available within families, ethnic groups and communities, which can be built upon to help safeguard children and promote their welfare.

7.26 Professionals should guard against myths and stereotypes – both positive and negative – of black and minority ethnic families. Anxiety about being accused of racist practice should not prevent the necessary action being taken to safeguard a child. Careful assessment – based on evidence – of a child's needs, and a family's strengths and weaknesses, understood in the context of the wider social environment, will help to avoid any distorting effect of these influences on professional judgements.

Sharing Information

General

7.27 Research and experience have shown repeatedly that keeping children safe from harm requires professionals and others to share information: about a child's health and development and exposure to possible harm; about a parent who may need help to, or may not be able to, care for a child adequately and safely; and about those who may pose a risk of harm to a child. Often, it is only when information from a number of sources has been shared and is then put together that it becomes clear that a child is at risk of or is suffering harm.

7.28 Those providing services to adults and children will be concerned about the need to balance their duties to protect children from harm and their general duty towards their patient or service user. Some professionals and staff face the added dimension of being involved in caring for, or supporting, more than one family member – the abused child, siblings, an alleged abuser. Where there are concerns that a child is, or may be at risk of significant harm, however, the needs of that child must come first. In these circumstances, the overriding objective must be to safeguard the child. In addition, there is a need for all agencies to hold information securely.

The Legal Framework

7.29 Professionals can only work together to safeguard children if there is an exchange of relevant information between them. This has been recognised in principle by the courts (see comments by Butler Sloss LJ in Re G (a minor) [1996] 2 All ER 65 at 68)[6]. Any disclosure of personal information to others must always, however, have regard to both common and statute law.

7.30 Normally, personal information should only be disclosed to third parties (including other agencies) with the consent of the subject of that information. Wherever possible, consent should be obtained before sharing personal information with third parties. In some circumstances, consent may not be possible or desirable but the safety and welfare of a child dictate that the information should be shared.

7.31 The best way of ensuring that information sharing is properly handled is to work within carefully worked out information sharing protocols between the agencies and

---

6. "The *Working Together* booklet does not have any legal status, but with the lesson of *Cleveland CCVF* in mind, the emphasis upon co-operation, joint investigation and full consultation at all stages of any investigation are crucial to the success of the government guidelines...The consequences of inter-agency co-operation is that there has to be free exchange of information between social workers and police officers together engaged in an investigation...The information obtained by social workers in the course of their duties is however confidential and covered by the umberella of public interest immunity...It can however be disclosed to fellow members of the child protection team engaged in the investigation of possible abuse of the child concerned."

professionals involved, and taking legal advice in individual cases where necessary. The Data Protection Registrar has produced a checklist for setting up information sharing arrangements which is reproduced at Appendix 4.

The Common Law Duty of Confidence

7.32 Personal information about children and families held by professionals and agencies is subject to a legal duty of confidence, and should not normally be disclosed without the consent of the subject. However, the law permits the disclosure of confidential information necessary to safeguard a child or children in the public interest: that is, the public interest in child protection may override the public interest in maintaining confidentiality. Disclosure should be justifiable in each case, according to the particular facts of the case, and legal advice should be sought in cases of doubt.

7.33 Children are entitled to the same duty of confidence as adults, provided that, in the case of those under 16 years of age, they have the ability to understand the choices and their consequences relating to any treatment. In exceptional circumstances, it may be believed that a child seeking advice, for example on sexual matters, is being exploited or abused. In such cases, confidentiality may be breached, following discussion with the child.

The Data Protection Act

7.34 The Data Protection Act 1998 requires that personal information is obtained and processed fairly and lawfully; only disclosed in appropriate circumstances; is accurate, relevant and not held longer than necessary; and is kept securely. The Act allows for disclosure without the consent of the subject in certain conditions, including for the purposes of the prevention or detection of crime, or the apprehension or prosecution of offenders, and where failure to disclose would be likely to prejudice those objectives in a particular case.

The European Convention on Human Rights

7.35 Article 8 of the European Convention on Human Rights states that:
   (1) Everyone has the right to respect for his private and family life, his home and his correspondence.
   (2) There shall be no interference by a public authority with the exercise of this right except such as in accordance with the law and is necessary in a democratic society in the interests of national security, public safety or the economic well-being of the country, for the prevention of disorder or crime, for the protection of health or morals, or for the protection of the rights and freedoms of others.

7.36 Disclosure of information without consent might give rise to an issue under Article 8. Disclosure of information to safeguard children will usually be for the protection of health or morals, for the protection of the rights and freedoms of others and for the prevention of disorder or crime. Disclosure should be appropriate for the purpose and only to the extent necessary to achieve that purpose.

Disclosure of Information about Sex Offenders

7.37 The Home Office has produced guidance[7] on the exchange of information about all those who have been convicted of, cautioned for, or otherwise dealt with by the courts for a sexual offence; and those who are considered by the relevant agencies to present a

---

7. *Draft Guidance on the Disclosure of Information about Sex Offenders who may present a risk to Children and Vulnerable adults.* Home Office, July 1999.

risk to children and others. The guidance also addresses issues arising in relation to people who have not been convicted or cautioned for offences, but who are suspected of involvement in criminal sexual activity.

7.38 The guidance emphasises that the disclosure of information should always take place within an established system and protocol between agencies, and should be integrated into a risk assessment and management system. Each case should be judged on its merits by the police and other relevant agencies, taking account of the degree of risk. The guidance places on the police the responsibility to co-ordinate and lead the risk assessment and management process. It advises that agencies should work within carefully worked out information sharing protocols, and refers to good practice material in existence. It also advocates the establishment of multi-agency risk panels whose purpose is to share information about offenders and to devise strategies to manage their risk.

Professional Guidance

Medical

7.39 The General Medical Council (GMC) has produced guidance entitled *Confidentiality* (1995). It emphasises the importance in most circumstances of obtaining a patient's consent to the disclosure of personal information, but makes clear that information may be released to third parties – if necessary without consent – in certain circumstances. Those circumstances include the following[8]:

Disclosure in the patient's medical interests

7.40 "Problems may arise if you consider that patient is incapable of giving consent to treatment because of immaturity, illness, or mental incapacity, and you have tried unsuccessfully to persuade the patient to allow an appropriate person to be involved in the consultation. If you are convinced that it is essential in the patient's medical interests, you may disclose relevant information to an appropriate person or authority. You must tell the patient before disclosing any information. You should remember that the judgement of whether patients are capable of giving or withholding consent to treatment or disclosure must be based on an assessment of their ability to appreciate what the treatment or advice being sought may involve, and not solely on their age. (para. 10)

7.41 "If you believe a patient to be a victim of neglect or physical or sexual abuse, and unable to give or withhold consent to disclosure, you should usually give this information to an appropriate responsible person or statutory agency, in order to prevent further harm to the patient. In these and similar circumstances, you may release information without the patient's consent, but only if you consider that the patient is unable to give consent, and that the disclosure is in the patient's best medical interests." (para. 11)

Disclosure in the interests of others

7.42 "Disclosures may be necessary in the public interest where a failure to disclose information may expose the patient, or others, to risk of death or serious harm. In such circumstances you should disclose the information promptly to an appropriate person or authority." (para. 18)

7.43 The GMC has confirmed that its guidance on the disclosure of information which may assist in the prevention or detection of abuse, applies both to information about third

---

8. Relevant extracts which should be read in the context of the full document.

parties (e.g. adults who may pose a risk of harm to a child), and about children who may be the subject of abuse.

Nursing

7.44   The United Kingdom Central Council for Nursing, Midwifery and Health Visiting (UKCC) has produced *Guidelines for professional practice* (1996), which contains the following advice on providing information[9]:

7.45   "Disclosure of information occurs:

* with the consent of the patient or client;

* without the consent of the patient or client when the disclosure is required by law or by order of a court; *and*

* without the consent of the patient or client when the disclosure is considered to be necessary in the public interest.

7.46   The public interest means the interests of an individual, or groups of individuals or of society as a whole and would, for example, cover matters such as serious crime, child abuse, drug trafficking or other activities which place others at serious risk (paras. 55–56)."

Record Keeping

7.47   Good record keeping is an important part of the accountability of professionals to those who use their services. It helps to focus work, and it is essential to working effectively across agency and professional boundaries. Clear and accurate records ensure that there is a documented account of an agency's or professional's involvement with a child and/or family. They help with continuity when individual workers are unavailable or change, and they provide an essential tool for managers to monitor work or for peer review. Records are an essential source of evidence for investigations and inquiries, and may also be required to be disclosed in court proceedings. Cases where enquiries do not result in the substantiation of referral concerns should be retained in accordance with agency record retention policies. These policies should ensure that records are stored safely and can be retrieved promptly and efficiently.

7.48   To serve these purposes, records should use clear, straightforward language, should be concise, and should be accurate not only in fact, but also in differentiating between opinion, judgements and hypothesis.

7.49   Well kept records provide an essential underpinning to good child protection practice. Safeguarding children requires information to be brought together from a number of sources and careful professional judgements to be made on the basis of this information. Records should be clear, accessible and comprehensive, with judgements made, and actions and decisions taken being carefully recorded. Where decisions have been taken jointly across agencies, or endorsed by a manager, this should be made clear.

7.50   Relevant information about a child and family who are the subject of child protection concerns will normally be collated in one place by the social services department. Records should readily tell the 'story' of a case. Specifically, the reader should be able to track:

* the relevant history of the child and family which led to the intervention;

* the nature of interventions, including intended outcomes;

* the means by which change is to be achieved; *and*

* the progress which is being made.

---

9. Relevant extracts which should be read in the context of the full document.

7.51 Agencies should consider which other agencies and professionals need to be informed about relevant changes of circumstances, for example the change of GP of a child whose name is on the child protection register. Each agency should ensure that when a child moves outside of their area, the child's records are transferred promptly to the relevant agency within the new area.

Supervision and Support

7.52 Working in the field of child protection entails making difficult and risky professional judgements. It is demanding work that can be distressing and stressful. All of those involved should have access to advice and support, from peers, managers, named and designated professionals, etc.

7.53 For many practitioners involved in day to day work with children and families, effective supervision is important to promoting good standards of practice and to supporting individual staff members. Supervision should help to ensure that practice is soundly based and consistent with ACPC and organisational procedures. It should ensure that practitioners fully understand their roles, responsibilities and the scope of their professional discretion and authority. It should also help identify the training and development needs of practitioners, so that each has the skills to provide an effective service.

7.54 Supervision should include scrutinising and evaluating the work carried out, assessing the strengths and weaknesses of the practitioner and providing coaching development and pastoral support. Supervisors should be available to practitioners as an important source of advice and expertise and may be required to endorse judgements at certain key points in child protection processes. Supervisors should also record key decisions within case records.

The Recruitment and Selection of Staff

7.55 All agencies and organisations whose staff, volunteers or foster carers work closely with children should have policies and procedures in place to deter those who are unsuitable to work with children. Common features should include the following:

* criminal record checks[10] (these may also be relevant for those with responsibilities for children, such as school governors and local authority councillors)

* for relevant organisations, checks of lists maintained by the Department of Health and the Department for Education and Employment, of those deemed unsuitable to work with children[11];

* checks of professional registers, if relevant;

* asking candidates to confirm identity through official documents;

* verifying the authenticity of qualifications and references directly;

* seeking a full employment history for prospective staff members and foster carers and reserving the right to approach any previous employer; checking with former

---

10. At the time of publication, police checks are available only for those in statutory and certain voluntary agencies who have 'substantial unsupervised access to children'. The establishment of the Criminal Records Bureau will provide a single point of reference for checking criminal records for employment purposes, and for accessing the lists held by the Department of Health and the Department for Education and Employment of those deemed unsuitable to work with children. Access to this information will be widened through the implementation of Part V of the Police Act 1997.

11. The Protection of Children Act 1999 requires regulated organisations not to offer child care work to anyone so listed. Further information is at Appendix 3.

employers the reason why employment ended; identifying any gaps or inconsistencies and seeking an explanation;

- making appointments only after references are obtained and checked. Referees should be reminded that references should contain no material mis-statement or omission relevant to the suitability of the applicant; *and*

- making all appointments to work with children (including internal transfers) subject to a probationary period.

7.56 Interviewers should be prepared to explore with candidates their attitudes towards children and childcare, their perceptions about the boundaries of acceptable behaviour towards children, and questions about sexual boundaries and attitudes.

7.57 Even the most careful selection process can not identify all those who may pose a risk to children. Post-employment management and supervision should always be alert to indicators of untoward behaviour.

8

Case reviews

Introduction

8.1   When a child dies, and abuse or neglect are known or suspected to be a factor in the death, local agencies should consider immediately whether there are other children at risk of harm who need safeguarding (e.g. siblings, other children in an institution where abuse is alleged). Thereafter, agencies should consider whether there are any lessons to be learned from the tragedy about the ways in which they work together to safeguard children. Consequently, when a child dies in such circumstances, the ACPC should always conduct a review into the involvement with the child and family of agencies and professionals. Additionally, ACPCs should always consider whether a review should be conducted where a child sustains a potentially life-threatening injury or serious and permanent impairment of health and development, or has been subjected to particularly serious sexual abuse; and the case gives rise to concerns about inter-agency working to protect children.

The Purpose of Reviews

8.2   The purpose of case reviews carried out under this guidance (known widely as 'Part 8 reviews') is to:

- establish whether there are lessons to be learned from the case about the way in which local professionals and agencies work together to safeguard children;
- identify clearly what those lessons are, how they will be acted upon, and what is expected to change as a result; and as a consequence, and
- to improve inter-agency working and better safeguard children.

8.3   Case reviews are not enquiries into how a child died or who is culpable; that is a matter for Coroners and Criminal Courts respectively to determine, as appropriate.

When Should an ACPC Undertake a Case Review?

8.4   Where more than one ACPC has knowledge of a child, the ACPC for the area in which the child is/was normally resident should take lead responsibility for conducting any review. Any other ACPCs that have an interest or involvement in the case should be included as partners in jointly planning and undertaking the review. In the case of looked after children, the responsible authority should exercise lead responsibility for conducting any review, again involving other ACPCs with an interest or involvement.

8.5   An ACPC should always undertake a case review when a child dies (including death by suicide), and abuse or neglect is known or suspected to be a factor in the child's death.

8.6 An ACPC should always consider whether to undertake a case review where a child has sustained a potentially life-threatening injury through abuse or neglect, serious sexual abuse, or sustained serious and permanent impairment of health or development through abuse or neglect, and the case gives rise to concerns about the way in which local professionals and services work together to safeguard children.

8.7 Any agency or professional may refer such a case to the ACPC Chair if it is believed that there are important lessons for inter-agency working to be learned from the case. In addition, the Secretary of State for Health has powers to demand an inquiry be held into the exercise of social services functions under s.81 of the Children Act 1989.

8.8 The following questions may help in deciding whether or not a case should be the subject of a case review in circumstances other than when a child dies – a 'yes' answer to several of these questions is likely to indicate that a review will yield useful lessons:

- was there clear evidence of a risk of significant harm to a child, which was:
  - not recognised by agencies or professional in contact with the child or perpetrator *or*
  - not shared with others *or*
  - not acted upon appropriately?
- was the child abused in an institutional setting (e.g. school, nursery, family centre)?
- was the child abused while being looked after by the local authority?
- does one or more agency or professional consider that its concerns were not taken sufficiently seriously, or acted upon appropriately, by another?
- does the case indicate that there may be failings in one or more aspects of the local operation of formal child protection procedures, which go beyond the handling of this case?
- was the child's name on the child protection register or had it been previously on the child protection register?
- does the case appear to have implications for a range of agencies and/or professionals?
- does the case suggest that the ACPC may need to change its local protocols or procedures, or that protocols and procedures are not adequately being promulgated, understood or acted upon?

Instigating a Case Review

Does the Case Meet Case Review Criteria?

8.9 The ACPC should first decide whether or not a case should be the subject of a case review, applying the criteria at paras. 8.5 and 8.6 above. ACPCs should establish a Serious Cases Review Panel involving as a minimum social services, health, education and the police to consider whether a case review should take place. In some cases, it may be valuable to conduct individual management reviews, or smaller-scale audits of individual cases which give rise to concern but which do not meet the criteria for a full case review. In such cases, arrangements should be made to share relevant findings with the Review Panel.

8.10 The Review Panel's decision should be forwarded as a recommendation to the Chair of the ACPC, who has ultimate responsibility for deciding whether or not to conduct a case review. Local authorities should always inform the Department of Health (through the SSI Social Care Region) of every case that becomes the subject of a case review.

Determining The Scope of The Review

8.11 The Review Panel should consider, in the light of each case, the scope of the review process, and draw up clear terms of reference. Relevant issues include:

- what appear to be the most important issues to address in trying to learn from this specific case? How can the relevant information best be obtained and analysed?

- are there features of the case which indicate that any part of the review process should involve, or be conducted by, a party independent of the professionals/agencies who will be required to participate in the review? Might it help the review panel to bring in an outside expert at any stage, to shed light on crucial aspects of the case?

- over what time period should events be reviewed, i.e. how far back should enquiries cover, and what is the cut-off point? What family history/background information will help better to understand the recent past and present which the review should try and capture?

- which agencies and professionals should contribute to the review, and who else (e.g. proprietor of independent school, playgroup leader) should be asked to submit reports or otherwise contribute?

- should family members be invited to contribute to the review?

- will the case gives rise to other parallel investigations of practice, for example, a mental health homicide or suicide enquiry, and if so, how can a co-ordinated review process best address all the relevant questions which need to be asked, in the most economical way?

- is there a need to involve agencies/professionals in other ACPC areas (see 8.4 above), and what should be the respective roles and responsibilities of the different ACPCs with an interest?

- how should the review process take account of a Coroner's enquiry, and (if relevant) any criminal investigations or proceedings related to the case? Is there a need to liaise with the Coroner and/or the Crown Prosecution Service?

- who will make the link with relevant interests outside the main statutory agencies, e.g. independent professionals, independent schools, voluntary organisations?

- when should the review process start and by what date should it be completed?

- how should any public, family and media interest be handled, before, during, and after the review?

- does the ACPC need to obtain independent legal advice about any aspect of the proposed review?

8.12 Some of these issues may need to be re-visited as the review progresses and new information emerges.

Timing

8.13 Reviews will vary widely in their breadth and complexity, but in all cases lessons should be learned and acted upon as quickly as possible. Within one month of a case coming to the attention of the ACPC Chair, there should be a Review Panel discussion to advise on whether a review should take place and subsequently to draw up terms of reference. Individual agencies should secure case records promptly and begin work quickly to draw up a chronology of involvement with the child and family.

8.14 Reviews should be completed within a further four months, unless an alternative timescale is agreed with the SSI Social Care Region at the outset. Sometimes the complexity of a case does not become apparent until the review is in progress. As soon as it emerges that a review cannot be completed within four months of the ACPC Chair's decision to initiate it, there should be a discussion with SSI Social Care Region to agree a timescale for completion.

8.15 In some cases, criminal proceedings may follow the death or serious injury of a child. Those co-ordinating the review should discuss with the relevant criminal justice agencies how the review process should take account of such proceedings, e.g. how does this affect timing, the way in which the review is conducted (including interviews of relevant personnel), and who should contribute at what stage? Case reviews should not be delayed as a matter of course because of outstanding criminal proceedings or an outstanding decision on whether or not to prosecute. Much useful work to understand and learn from the features of the case can often proceed without risk of contamination of witnesses in criminal proceedings. In some cases, it may not be possible to complete or to publish a review until after Coroners or criminal proceedings have been concluded but this should not prevent early lessons learned from being implemented.

Who Should Conduct Reviews?

8.16 The initial scoping of the review should identify those who should contribute, although it may emerge, as information becomes available, that the involvement of others would be useful. In particular, information may become available through criminal proceedings, which may be of relevance to the review.

8.17 Each relevant service should undertake a separate management review of its involvement with the child and family. This should begin as soon as a decision is taken to proceed with a review, and even sooner if a case gives rise to concerns within the individual agency. Relevant independent professionals (including GPs) should contribute reports of their involvement. Designated professionals should review and evaluate the practice of all involved health professionals and providers within a health authority area. This may involve reviewing the involvement of individual practitioners and Trusts and also advising named professionals and managers who are compiling reports for the review. Designated professionals have an important role in providing guidance on how to balance confidentiality and disclosure issues. The GALRO service is expected to contribute to the review, when felt appropriate by the ACPC, and should facilitate contributions. Where a *guardian ad litem* contributes to a review, the prior agreement of the courts should be sought so that the guardian's duty of confidentiality under the court rules can be waived to the degree necessary.

8.18 The ACPC should commission an overview report which brings together and analyses the findings of the various reports from agencies and others, and which makes recommendations for future action.

8.19 Those conducting management reviews of individual services, or producing the overview report, should not have been directly concerned with the child or family, or the immediate line manager of the practitioner(s) involved.

Individual Management Reviews

8.20 Once it is known that a case is being considered for review, each agency should secure records relating to the case to guard against loss or interference.

8.21 The aim of management reviews should be to look openly and critically at individual and organisational practice to see whether the case indicates that changes could and should be made, and if so, to identify how those changes will be brought about.

Management review reports should be accepted by the senior officer in the agency who has commissioned the report and who will be responsible for ensuring that recommendations are acted upon.

8.22 Upon completion of the review report, there should be a process for feedback and debriefing for staff involved, in advance of completion of the overview report by the ACPC. There may also be a need for a follow-up feedback session if the ACPC overview report raises new issues for the agency and staff members.

8.23 Case reviews are not a part of any disciplinary enquiry or process, but information that emerges in the course of reviews may indicate that disciplinary action should be taken under established procedures. Alternatively, reviews may be conducted concurrently with disciplinary action. In some cases (e.g. alleged institutional abuse) disciplinary action may be needed urgently to safeguard other children.

8.24 The following outline format should guide the preparation of management reviews, to help ensure that the relevant questions are addressed, and to provide information to ACPCs in a consistent format to help with preparing an overview report. The questions posed do not comprise a comprehensive check-list relevant to all situations. Each case may give rise to specific questions or issues which need to be explored, and each review should consider carefully the circumstances of individual cases and how best to structure a review in the light of those particular circumstances. Where staff or others are interviewed by those preparing management reviews, a written record of such interviews should be made and this should be shared with the relevant interviewee.

The ACPC Overview Report

8.25 The ACPC overview report should bring together and relate the information and analysis contained in the individual management reviews, together with reports commissioned from any other relevant interests. Overview reports should be produced according to the following outline format although, as with management reviews, the precise format will depend upon the features of the case. This outline will be most relevant to abuse or neglect which has taken place in a family setting.

ACPC Action on Receiving Reports

8.26 On receiving an overview report the ACPC should:

* ensure that contributing agencies and individuals are satisfied that their information is fully and fairly represented in the overview report;

* translate recommendations into an action plan which should be endorsed and adopted at a senior level by each of the agencies involved. The plan should set out who will do what, by when, and with what intended outcome. The plan should set out by what means improvements in practice/systems will be monitored and reviewed;

* clarify to whom the report, or any part of it, should be made available;

* disseminate report or key findings to interests as agreed. Make arrangements to provide feedback and de-briefing to staff, family members of the subject child, and the media, as appropriate; *and*

* provide a copy of the overview report, executive summary action plan and individual management reports to the Department of Health (SSI Social Care Region).

Reviewing Institutional Abuse

8.27 When serious abuse takes place in an institution, or multiple abusers are involved, the same principles of review apply. However, they are likely to be more complex, on a larger scale, and may require more time. Terms of reference need to be carefully constructed to explore the issues relevant to the specific case. For example, if children had been abused in a residential school, it would be important to explore whether and how the school had taken steps to create a safe environment for children, and to respond to specific concerns raised.

MANAGEMENT REVIEWS

What Was Our Involvement with This Child and Family?

Construct a comprehensive chronology of involvement by the agency and/or professional(s) in contact with the child and family over the period of time set out in the review's terms of reference. Briefly summarise decisions reached, the services offered and/or provided to the child(ren) and family, and other action taken.

Analysis of Involvement

Consider the events that occurred, the decisions made, and the actions taken or not. Where judgements were made, or actions taken, which indicate that practice or management could be improved, try to get an understanding not only of what happened, but why. Consider specifically:

- Were practitioners sensitive to the needs of the children in their work, knowledgeable about potential indicators of abuse or neglect, and about what to do if they had concerns about a child?
- Did the agency have in place policies and procedures for safeguarding children and acting on concerns about their welfare?
- What were the key relevant points/opportunities for assessment and decision making in this case in relation to the child and family? Do assessments and decisions appear to have been reached in an informed and professional way?
- Did actions accord with assessments and decisions made? Were appropriate services offered/provided, or relevant enquiries made, in the light of assessments?
- Where relevant, were appropriate child protection or care plans in place, and child protection and/or looked after reviewing processes complied with?
- When, and in what way, were the child(ren)'s wishes and feelings ascertained and considered? Was this information recorded?
- Was practice sensitive to the racial, cultural, linguistic and religious identity of the child and family?
- Were more senior managers, or other agencies and professionals, involved at points where they should have been?
- Was the work in this case consistent with agency and ACPC policy and procedures for safeguarding children, and wider professional standards?

What Do We Learn From This Case?

Are there lessons from this case for the way in which this agency works to safeguard children and promote their welfare? Is there good practice to highlight, as well as ways in which practice can be improved? Are there implications for ways of working; training (single and inter-agency); management and supervision; working in partnership with other agencies; resources?

Recommendations for Action

What action should be taken by whom, and by when? What outcomes should these actions bring about, and how will the agency review whether they have been achieved?

ACPC OVERVIEW REPORT

Introduction

- Summarise the circumstances that led to a review being undertaken in this case.
- State terms of reference of review.
- List contributors to the review and the nature of their contributions (e.g. management review by LEA, report from adult mental health service). List review panel members and author of overview report.

The Facts

- Prepare a genogram showing membership of family, extended family and household.
- Compile an integrated chronology of involvement with the child and family on the part of all relevant agencies, professionals and others who have contributed to the review process. Note specifically in the chronology each occasion on which the child was seen and the child's views and wishes sought or expressed.
- Prepare an overview which summarises what relevant information was known to the agencies and professionals involved, about the parents/carers, any perpetrator, and the home circumstances of the children.

Analysis

This part of the overview should look at how and why events occurred, decisions were made, actions taken or not. This is the part of the report in which reviewers can consider, with the benefit of hindsight, whether different decisions or actions may have led to an alternative course of events. The analysis section is also where any examples of good practice should be highlighted.

Conclusions and Recommendations

This part of the report should summarise what, in the opinion of the review panel, are the lessons to be drawn from the case and how those lessons should be translated into recommendations for action. Recommendations should include, but not be limited to, the recommendations made in individual agency reports. Recommendations should be few in number, focused and specific, and capable of being implemented. If there are lessons for national, as well as local, policy and practice these should also be highlighted.

8.28 There needs to be clarity over the interface between the different processes of investigation (including criminal investigations); case management, including help for abused children and immediate measures to ensure that other children are safe; and review, i.e. learning lessons from the case to lessen the likelihood of such events happening again. The different processes should inform each other. Any proposals for review should be agreed with those leading criminal investigations, to make sure that they do not prejudice possible criminal proceedings.

Accountability and Disclosure

8.29 ACPCs should consider carefully who might have an interest in reviews – e.g. elected and appointed members of authorities, staff, members of the child's family, the public, the media – and what information should be made available to each of these interests. There are difficult interests to balance, among them:

- the need to maintain confidentiality in respect of personal information contained within reports on the child, family members and others;

- the accountability of public services and the importance of maintaining public confidence in the process of internal review;

- the need to secure full and open participation from the different agencies and professionals involved;

- the responsibility to provide relevant information to those with a legitimate interest; *and*

- constraints on sharing information when criminal proceedings are outstanding, in that access to the contents of information may not be within the control of the ACPC.

8.30   It is important to anticipate requests for information and plan in advance how they should be met. For example, a lead agency may take responsibility for de-briefing family members, or for responding to media interest about a case, in liaison with contributing agencies and professionals. In all cases, the ACPC overview report should contain an executive summary that will be made public, which includes as a minimum, information about the review process, key issues arising from the case and the recommendations which have been made. Such publication will need to be timed in accordance with the conclusion of any related court proceedings. The content will need to be suitably anonymised in order to protect the confidentiality of relevant family members and others.

Learning Lessons Locally

8.31   Reviews are of little value unless lessons are learned from them. At least as much effort should be spent on acting upon recommendations as on conducting the review. The following may help in getting maximum benefit from the review process:

- as far as possible, conduct the review in such a way that the process is a learning exercise in itself, rather than a trial or ordeal;

- consider what information needs to be disseminated, how and to whom, in the light of a review. Be prepared to communicate examples of both good practice and areas where change is required;

- focus recommendations on a small number of key areas, with specific and achievable proposals for change and intended outcomes;

- the ACPC should put in place a means of auditing action against recommendations and intended outcomes;

- seek feedback on review reports from the Department of Health SSI Social Care Region who should use reports to inform inspections and performance management.

8.32   Day to day good practice can help ensure that reviews are conducted successfully and in a way most likely to maximise learning:

- establish a culture of audit and review. Make sure that tragedies are not the only reason inter-agency work is reviewed;

- have in place clear, systematic case recording and record keeping systems;

- develop good communication and mutual understanding between disciplines and ACPC members;

- communicate with the local community and media to raise awareness of the positive and 'helping' work of statutory services with children, so that attention is not focused disproportionately on tragedies;

- make sure staff and their representatives understand what can be expected in the event of a child death/case review.

Learning Lessons Nationally

8.33 Taken together, case reviews are an important source of information to inform national policy and practice. The Department of Health is responsible for identifying and disseminating common themes and trends across review reports, and acting on lessons for policy and practice. The Department of Health commissions overview reports at least every two years, drawing out key findings of case reviews and their implications for policy and practice.

96

9

Inter-agency training and development

Introduction

9.1 Professional staff who come into contact with children should know of the predisposing factors and signs and indicators of child abuse. They should be able to exercise professional skill in terms of effective information sharing and the ability to analyse this information. They should also have the knowledge and skills to collaborate with other agencies and disciplines in order to safeguard the welfare of children. Those involved in child protection work also need a sound understanding of the legislative framework and the wider policy context within which they work, as well as a familiarity with local policy and procedures. Individual agencies are responsible for ensuring that their staff are competent and confident to carry out their child protection responsibilities.

9.2 Inter-agency training should complement the training available to staff in single agency or professional settings. It can be a highly effective way of promoting a common and shared understanding of the respective roles and responsibilities of different professionals and can contribute to effective working relationships.

9.3 Training should create an ethos which values working collaboratively with other professionals, respects diversity (including culture, race and disability), is child-centred, promotes partnership with children and families and recognises families' strengths in responding to the needs of their children.

9.4 Inter-agency training should focus on the way in which those engaged in child welfare work with others to meet the needs of children. This training should complement the training available to staff in single agency settings.

Target Audience

9.5 Inter-agency training should be targeted at the following groups from voluntary, statutory and independent agencies:

- those who work directly with children in need, e.g. GPs, hospital and community health staff, family centre workers, teachers, Education Welfare Officers, social workers (including residential and day care staff) and foster carers;
- those who work in adult services relevant to children's welfare (e.g. mental health and learning disability staff, probation officers);
- those who supervise staff and volunteers in the above groups;
- those who have a strategic and managerial responsibility for commissioning and delivering services for children and families, including school governors and trustees; *and*

- all those who come into contact with or provide services to children, for example day care staff, police, housing, leisure services and youth service staff all need introductory training on safeguarding children, including the importance of inter-agency collaboration.

9.6 Individual employers are responsible for ensuring that continuing professional development is provided to enable employees in the above target groups, to develop and maintain the necessary knowledge, values and skills to work together to safeguard children. Employers should ensure that their staff are aware of indicators of abuse, and safe practice within their work setting before attending inter-agency training.

The Purpose of Inter-Agency Training

9.7 The purpose of inter-agency training is to help develop and foster the following in order to achieve better outcomes for children:

- a shared understanding of the tasks, processes, principles, roles and responsibilities and local arrangements for safeguarding children and promoting their welfare;

- co-ordinated services at both the strategic and individual case level;

- improved communications between professionals including a common understanding of key terms, definitions and thresholds for action;

- effective working relationships, based on respect and an understanding of the role and contribution of different disciplines; *and*

- sound decision making based on information sharing, thorough assessment, critical analysis and professional judgement.

Training in Context

9.8 Inter-agency training can only be fully effective if it is embedded within a wider framework of commitment to inter-agency working, underpinned by shared goals, planning processes and values. It is most likely to be effective if it is delivered within a framework that includes:

- a clear mandate from senior managers;

- standards of practice;

- policies and procedures and practice guidelines to inform and support these standards;

- a training needs analysis based on identifying needs using standards for practice; *and*

- a training strategy that makes clear the difference between single agency and inter-agency training responsibilities.

The Role of the ACPC

9.9 The ACPC is responsible for taking a strategic overview of the planning, delivery and evaluation of the inter-agency training that is required in order to promote effective practice to safeguard the welfare of children.

9.10 Effective high quality training is most likely to be achieved if the ACPC is strategically involved at all stages of the training cycle. This includes:

- ensuring training needs are identified and met within the context of local and national policy and practice developments. This should be achieved by an established system for identifying training needs, and systems for the co-ordination and management of training delivery and evaluation;

- developing and maintaining structures and processes for an organised and co-ordinated approach to inter-agency training. Experience suggests that this is best achieved by establishing, maintaining and supporting an ACPC training sub-committee. Training needs to be informed by policy and practice developments at both a national and local level; *and*

- including training as a standard ACPC agenda item. Regular consideration should be given by the ACPC to ensuring that: recommendations regarding inter-agency training within the area are based on local and national needs; training reflects current ACPC strategies; and single and inter-agency training responsibilities are negotiated and agreed upon.

The Role of the Training Sub-Committee

9.11 The ACPC training sub-committee is responsible for inter-agency training through overseeing and managing its planning, design, delivery, and evaluation. If it is to be effective, the training sub-committee should include representatives of statutory, voluntary and independent agencies whose staff need training for inter-agency practice. It should also include members with sufficient knowledge of training processes to enable them to make informed decisions regarding the development, implementation and evaluation of a training strategy.

Role of Employers

9.12 Employers have a responsibility to resource and support inter-agency training by:

- providing staff who have the relevant expertise to sit on the training sub-committee and contribute to training;

- allocating the time needed to complete inter-agency training tasks effectively;

- releasing staff to attend the appropriate inter-agency training courses, and ensuring that members of staff receive relevant in-house training which enables them to maximise the learning derived from inter-agency training. In addition, staff should have opportunities to consolidate learning from inter-agency training;

- contributing to the planning, resourcing, delivery and evaluation of training.

Audience, Levels and Outcomes of Training

9.13 Training should be available at a number of levels to address the learning needs of different staff. The following framework outlines three stages of training and matches them with target audiences who have different degrees of involvement or decision-making responsibility for children's welfare. Decisions should be made locally about how the stages are most appropriately delivered and this should form part of the ACPC's training strategy.

9.14 The detailed content of training at each level of the framework shown should be specified locally. The content should reflect the principles, values and processes set out in this guidance on work with children and families. Steps should be taken to ensure the relevance of the content to different professional groups from the statutory voluntary, and independent sectors. The content of training programmes should be regularly reviewed and updated in the light of research and practice experience.

9.15 There are significant numbers of people who are in contact with children away from their families, for example youth workers, child minders, those working with children in residential and day care settings and those working in sport and leisure settings in both a paid and unpaid capacity. All of these should, as a minimum, be provided with

Framework for Training to Promote Working Together[12]

Those involved in assessment and intervention to safeguard children ▶

Those who work directly with children, or adults who are parents ▶

Those in contact with children or parents ▶

Qualifying training

Introduction to working together to safeguard children	Working together: Foundation	Working together on particular practice
Key Outcomes	*Key Outcomes*	*Key Outcomes*
● Contribute and take whatever actions are needed to safeguard children.	● Accomplish core tasks together to safeguard and promote children's welfare e.g. assessments, planning, core groups, conferences, decision making.	● Co-work on complex tasks or particular areas of practice that have specific knowledge or skill requirements, e.g, joint enquiries and investigations, investigative interviews, complex assessments.
● Recognise and respond to concerns about a child in need.	● Sound understanding of principles and processes for effective collaboration.	● Establish and maintain partnerships of mutual trust and respect.
● Appreciate own role and that of others.	● Communicate and develop working relationships in the interests of children.	● Understand legal and organisational frameworks, including levels of accountability of decision making, in other agencies.
● Communicate and act appropriately within national and local guidance to safeguard children.	● Understand contribution made by others to safeguarding children and impact of own decisions and actions on others.	
● Familiar with local arrangements, services and sources of advice for supporting families and safeguarding children.		

In addition managers need appropriate training to enable these outcomes to be achieved

an introductory level of training on safeguarding children. Given the large numbers and work patterns of those involved, creative methods should be used to provide them with the essential training. For example, open learning materials may be helpful, or the inclusion of designated people from community or religious groups within ACPC training, who are able to support others using open learning materials or to facilitate training within their own organisation.

9.16 Managers at all levels, within organisations employing staff to work with children and families, benefit from specific training on inter-agency practice to safeguard children. Practice supervisors, professional advisers/designated child protection specialists and service managers need not only a foundation level of training, but may also need training on joint planning and commissioning, managing joint services and teams; chairing multi-disciplinary meetings; negotiating joint protocols and mediating where there is conflict and difference. Specific training on the conduct of case reviews will be relevant to some.

9.17 ACPCs should consider their own collective development needs as a group. There are significant benefits to be derived from periodically undertaking facilitated development work in order to improve effectiveness.

---

12. Charles M, Hendry E (eds). *Training Together to Safeguard Children*. London: NSPCC (In press).

9.18 A number of ACPCs have undertaken innovative public education programmes to increase community awareness, and to enable individuals to play their part in safeguarding children.

Systems for the Delivery of Inter-Agency Training

9.19 Systems should be established under the auspices of the ACPC. These should foster collaboration across agencies and disciplines in relation to planning, design, delivery and administration of the training. They should be efficient as well as being designed to promote co-operation and shared ownership of the training. Training may be delivered more effectively if ACPCs collaborate, especially where police or health boundaries embrace more than one ACPC.

9.20 The appointment of an Inter-agency Training Co-ordinator, funded by constituent members of the ACPC and reporting to the ACPC, has proved an effective approach for managing the planning, administration and delivery of training. It is only likely to be viable where an ACPC is sufficiently large to sustain such an appointment or where smaller ACPCs pool resources. Some areas maintain an inter-agency training panel of suitably skilled and experienced practitioners and managers from the ACPC constituent members who work together to assess training needs, design, deliver and evaluate inter-agency training. The effectiveness of this approach relies on having a skilled person to co-ordinate and develop the panel, and on the allocation of time to enable panel members to undertake this work.

Quality Assurance and Effectiveness

9.21 The ACPC, or the Training sub-committee acting on its behalf, has a responsibility to ensure that the training is delivered to a consistently high standard, and that a process exists for evaluation of training effectiveness. This responsibility includes ensuring that:

- the training is delivered by trainers who are knowledgeable about safeguarding children and have facilitation skills;

- all inter-agency training reflects understanding of rights of the children and is informed by an active respect for diversity, and a commitment to ensuring equality of opportunity;

- training is regularly evaluated to ensure that it meets the agreed learning outcomes; *and*

- the evaluation process informs the training strategy.

9.22 Training is most effective when those engaged in its planning, delivery and evaluation are aware of current policy and practice developments. Such a position might be achieved by:

- identifying training implications for all ACPC policy and practice developments;

- specifying training implications for all ACPC policy and practice developments;

- ensuring that subsequent training is informed by current research evidence, lessons from case reviews and local and national developments and initiatives.

Appendix

1

Framework for the Assessment of Children in Need and their Families

The *Framework for the Assessment of Children in Need and their Families* (outlined at Figure 1) provides a systematic basis for collecting and analysing information to support professional judgements about how to help children and families in the best interests of the child. Practitioners should use the framework to gain an understanding of a child's developmental needs; the capacity of parents or caregivers to respond appropriately to those needs, including their capacity to keep the child safe from harm; and the impact of wider family and environmental factors on the parents and child. Each of the three main aspects of the framework – the child's developmental needs; parenting capacity; and wider family and environmental factors – is outlined in more detail in Boxes 1, 2 and 3 respectively.

The framework is to be used within social services departments for the assessment of all children in need, including those where there are concerns that a child may be suffering significant harm. The process of engaging in an assessment should be viewed as being part of the range of services offered to children and families.

Use of the framework should provide evidence to help, guide and inform judgements about children's welfare and safety from the first point of contact, through the processes of initial and more detailed core assessments, according to the nature and extent of the child's needs. The provision of appropriate services need not and should not wait until the end of the assessment process, but should be determined according to what is required, and when, to promote the welfare and safety of the child.

Evidence about children's developmental progress – and their parents' capacity to respond appropriately to the child's needs within the wider family and environmental context – should underpin judgements about:

- the child's welfare and safety;
- whether, and if so how, to provide help to children and family members; *and*
- what form of intervention will bring about the best possible outcomes for the child, and what the intended outcomes of intervention are.

Figure 1 Assessment Framework

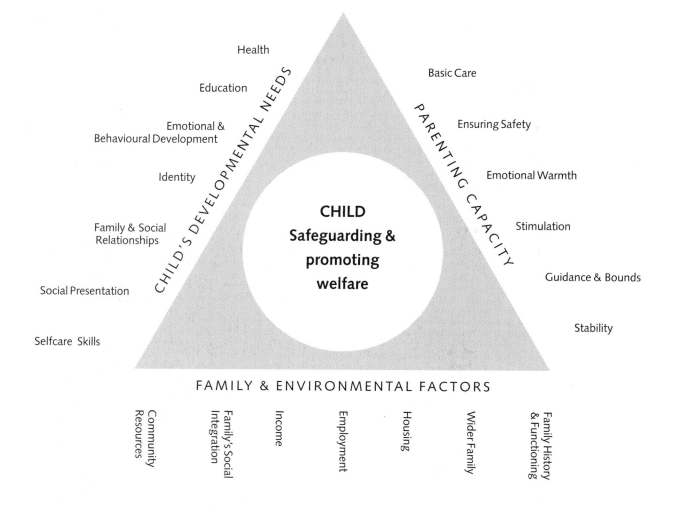

Box 1

DIMENSIONS OF CHILD'S DEVELOPMENTAL NEEDS

Health

Includes growth and development as well as physical and mental wellbeing. The impact of genetic factors and of any impairment need to be considered. Involves receiving appropriate health care when ill, an adequate and nutritious diet, exercise, immunisations where appropriate and developmental checks, dental and optical care and, for older children, appropriate advice and information on issues that have an impact on health, including sex education and substance misuse.

Education

Covers all areas of a child's cognitive development which begins from birth. Includes opportunities: for play and interaction with other children to have access to books; to acquire a range of skills and interests; to experience success and achievement. Involves an adult interested in educational activities, progress and achievements, who takes account of the child's starting point and any special educational needs.

Emotional and Behavioural Development

Concerns the appropriateness of response demonstrated in feelings and actions by a child, initially to parents and caregivers and, as the child grows older, to others beyond the family. Includes nature and quality of early attachments, characteristics of temperament, adaptation to change, response to stress and degree of appropriate self control.

Identity

Concerns the child's growing sense of self as a separate and valued person. Includes the child's view of self and abilities, self image and self esteem, and having a positive sense of individuality. Race religion, age, gender, sexuality and disability may all contribute to this. Feelings of belonging and acceptance by family, peer group and wider society, including other cultural groups.

Family and Social Relationships

Development of empathy and the capacity to place self in someone else's shoes. Includes a stable and affectionate relationship with parents or caregivers, good relationships with siblings, increasing importance of age appropriate friendships with peers and other significant persons in the child's life and response of family to these relationships.

Social Presentation

Concerns child's growing understanding of the way in which appearance, behaviour, and any impairment are perceived by the outside world and the impression being created. Includes appropriateness of dress for age, gender, culture and religion; cleanliness and personal hygiene; and availability of advice from parents or caregivers about presentation in different settings.

Self Care Skills

Concerns the acquisition by a child of practical, emotional and communication competencies required for increasing independence. Includes early practical skills of dressing and feeding, opportunities to gain confidence and practical skills to undertake activities away from the family and independent living skills as older children. Includes encouragement to acquire social problem solving approaches. Special attention should be given to the impact of a child's impairment and other vulnerabilities, and on social circumstances affecting these in the development of self care skills.

Box 2

DIMENSIONS OF PARENTING CAPACITY

Basic Care
Providing for the child's physical needs, and appropriate medical and dental care.

Includes provision of food, drinkn, warmth, shelter, clean and appropriate clothing and adequate personal hygiene.

Ensuring Safety
Ensuring the child is adequately protected from harm or danger.

Includes protection from significant harm or danger, and from contact with unsafe adults/other children and from self-harm. Recognition of hazards and danger both in the home and elsewhere.

Emotional Warmth
Ensuring the child's emotional needs are met giving the child a sense of being specially valued and a positive sense of own racial and cultural identity.

Includes ensuring the child's requirements for secure, stable and affectionate relationships with significant adults, with appropriate sensitivity and responsiveness to the child's needs. Appropriate physical contact, comfort and cuddling sufficient to demonstrate warm regard, praise and encouragement.

Stimulation
Promoting child's learning and intellectual development through encouragement and cognitive stimulation and promoting social opportunities.

Includes facilitating the child's cognitive development and potential through interaction, communication, talking and responding to the child's language and questions, encouraging and joining the child's play, and promoting educational opportunities. Enabling the child to experience success and ensuring school attendance or equivalent opportunity. Facilitating child to meet challenges of life.

Guidance and Boundaries
Enabling the child to regulate their own emotions and behaviour.

The key parental tasks are demonstrating and modelling appropriate behaviour and control of emotions and interactions with others, and guidance which involves setting boundaries, so that the child is able to develop an internal model of moral values and conscience, and social behaviour appropriate for the society within which they will grow up. The aim is to enable the child to grow into an autonomous adult, holding their own values, and able to demonstrate appropriate behaviour with others rather than having to be dependent on rules outside themselves. This includes not over protecting children from exploratory and learning experiences.

Includes social problem solving, anger management, consideration for others, and effective discipline and shaping of behaviour.

Stability
Providing a sufficiently stable family environment to enable a child to develop and maintain a secure attachment to the primary caregiver(s) in order to ensure optimal development. Includes: ensuring secure attachments are not disrupted, providing consistency of emotional warmth over time and responding in a similar manner to the same behaviour. Parental responses change and develop according to child's developmental progress. In addition, ensuring children keep in contact with important family members and significant others.

Box 3

FAMILY AND ENVIRONMENTAL FACTORS

Family History and Functioning
Family history includes both genetic and psycho-social factors.

Family functioning is influenced by who is living in the household and how they are related to the child; significant changes in family/household composition; history of childhood experiences of parents; chronology of significant life events and their meaning to family members; nature of family functioning, including sibling relationships and its impact on the child; parental strengths and difficulties, including those of an absent parent; the relationship between separated parents.

Wider Family
Who are considered to be members of the wider family by the child and the parents? This includes related and non-related persons and absent wider family. What is their role and importance to the child and parents and in precisely what way?

Housing
Does the accommodation have basic amenities and facilities appropriate to the age and development of the child and other resident members? Is the housing accessible and suitable to the needs of disabled family members? Includes the interior and exterior of the accommodation and immediate surroundings. Basic amenities include water, heating, sanitation, cooking facilities, sleeping arrangements and cleanliness, hygiene and safety and their impact on the child's upbringing.

Employment
Who is working in the household, their pattern of work and any changes? What impact does this have on the child? How is work or absence of work viewed by family members? How does it affect their relationship with the child? Includes children's experience of work and its impact on them.

Income
Income available over a sustained period of time. Is the family in receipt of all its benefit entitlements? Sufficiency of income to meet the family's needs. The way resources available to the family are used. Are there financial difficulties which affect the child?

Family's Social Integration
Exploration of the wider context of the local neighbourhood and community and its impact on the child and parents. Includes the degree of the family's integration or isolation, their peer groups, friendship and social networks and the importance attached to them.

Community Resources
Describes all facilities and services in a neighbourhood, including universal services of primary health care, day care and schools, places of worship, transport, shops and leisure activities. Includes availability, accessibility and standard of resources and impact on the family, including disabled members.

2

Appendix

Points of contact for armed forces arrangements for child protection

This Appendix offers points of contact for the relevant Service agencies in child protection matters.

Royal Navy

All child protection matters within the Royal Navy are managed by the Naval Personal and Family Service (NPFS), the Royal Navy's social work department. This provides a confidential and professional social work service to all Naval personnel and their families, liasing as appropriate with local authority social services departments. Child protection issues involving the family of a member of the Royal Navy should be referred to the relevant Area Officer, NPFS.

NPFS Eastern Area Portsmouth   (02392) 722712   Fax: 725803

NPFS Northern Area Helensburgh   (01436) 672798   Fax: 674965

NPFS Western Area Plymouth   (01752) 555041   Fax: 555647

Royal Marines

The Royal Marines Welfare Service is staffed by trained but unqualified Royal Marine senior non-commissioned officers (NCOs). They are accountable to a qualified social work manager at Headquarters Royal Marines, Portsmouth. For child protection matters involving Royal Marines families, social services departments should notify SO3 (WFS) at Portsmouth. Tel: (02392) 547542.

Army

The provision of welfare support to Army families in the UK is the responsibility of the Army Welfare Service (AWS). Where a child or children from an Army family are subject to a child protection investigation, contact should be made immediately with the SSAFA-FH social worker within the local Garrison AWS Personal Support Teams. In the event of difficulty, Social Services Departments should liaise directly with the SSAFA-FH Assistant Controller who acts on behalf of the Colonel, Army Welfare Service in these matters:

The Assistant Controller (Support Services) UK, HQ Land Command, Erskine Barracks, Wilton, Salisbury, Wiltshire SP2 0AG

Tel: (01722) 436563   Fax: (01722) 436307

Royal Air Force

Welfare support for families in the RAF is managed as a normal function of command and co-ordinated by each Station's Personnel Officer, the Officer Commanding Personnel Management Squadron (OCPMS) or the Officer Commanding

Administrative Squadron (OCA), depending on the size of the Station. A number of qualified SSAFA-FH social workers and social work assistants are employed to help.

Whenever a child protection investigation concerns the child of a serving member of the RAF, the relevant social services department should notify the parent's Unit, or, if this is not known, contact the OCPMS/OCA of the nearest RAF Unit. Every RAF Unit has an officer appointed to this duty who will be familiar with child protection procedures. Alternatively the SSAFA-FH Head of Service RAF can be contacted at:

Head of Service, SSAFA-FH Social Work Service RAF (UK), HQ Personnel and Training Command, RAF Innsworth, Gloucester, GL3 1EZ

Tel: (01452) 712612 Ext. 5815   Fax: (01452) 510875

Overseas

The following should be consulted:

Royal Navy

Area Officer (NPFS) Eastern, HMS Nelson, Queen Street, Portsmouth, PO1 3HH

Tel: (02392) 722712   Fax: (02392) 725083

Army and Royal Air Force

The Director of Social Work, SSAFA-Forces Help, 19 Queen Elizabeth Street, London SE1 2LP

Tel: 020 7403 8783   Fax: 020 7403 8815

The Protection of Children Act 1999

Purpose

The Act has four principal objectives:

- to make statutory the Department of Health's 'Consultancy Service Index' list[13], and to require regulated child care organisations – and permit other child care organisations – to refer for inclusion on a new list the names of individuals considered unsuitable to work with children;

- to provide rights of appeal against inclusion on both the Department of Health list and the Department for Education and Employment's 'List 99'[14] (which has always been a statutory list);

- to require regulated child care organisations to check the names of anyone they propose to employ in posts involving regular contact with children against both Departmental lists and not to employ if listed[15]; *and*

- to amend Part V of the Police Act 1997 to allow the Criminal Records Bureau to act as a central access point for criminal records information, List 99 and the new Department of Health list, i.e. to act as a 'one stop shop' for checks on those applying to work with children.

The Act also provides for an independent appeal system. A tribunal will examine the evidence afresh and make its own decision on the merits of the particular case.

Under the Act (Section 7), where a child care organisation proposes to offer employment in a child care position it needs to ascertain whether the individual is included in the list – and if so, not to offer him or her employment. For the purposes of the Act, a child care organisation is defined under Section 12 as:

[an organisation]:

- which is concerned with the provision of accommodation, social services or health services to children or the supervision of children.

- whose activities are regulated by or by virtue of any prescribed enactment; *and*

- which fulfils such other conditions as may be prescribed.

All childcare organisations as defined in the Act will be required to check the DH list in respect of prospective employees, paid or unpaid, for work involving contact with children. Other organisations, will be able to check prospective employees and volunteers against the DH list.

---

13. A list held by the Department of Health of those considered unsuitable to work with children.

14. A list held by the Department of Education and Employment of teachers and other education staff who are barred from employment in the education service.

15. In the case of List 99, only if listed on certain grounds.

Appendix

Data protection registrar's checklist for setting up information sharing arrangements
(abridged version)

(i) What is the purpose of the information sharing arrangement?

1. It is important in data protection terms that the purpose of any information sharing arrangement is clearly defined. This is because if *personal* information is to be disclosed, then disclosures must be registered with the Data Protection Registrar and the data protection principles will take effect. These principles themselves relate directly to the purpose or purposes for which personal information is held. For example, information must be adequate, relevant, and not excessive in relation to the purpose for which it is held, and must not be held longer than is necessary for that purpose.

2. Parties to any arrangement should be aware that under the Data Protection Act 1998 requires that there is a "legitimate basis" for disclosing sensitive personal data. The introduction of special controls on the processing of sensitive data (including holding and disclosing them) is one of the major innovations of the new Act. Under section 2, "sensitive data" include information as to the commission, or alleged commission, by the data subject of any offence; and criminal proceedings involving the data subject as the accused, and their disposal. The definition of "sensitive data" also includes information about the data subject's sexual life. It should also be made clear to all parties that information received under the arrangement is to be used only for the specified purpose(s). Thus, there should be a restriction on secondary use of personal data received under any information sharing arrangement *unless* the consent of the disclosing party to that secondary use is sought and granted.

(ii) Will it be necessary to share personal information in order to fulfil that purpose?

3. Depersonalised information is information presented in such a way that individuals cannot be identified. If depersonalised information can be used to achieve the purpose, then there will be no data protection implications. Consideration should therefore always be given to whether the purpose can be achieved using depersonalised information; "would failure to share personal information mean that the objectives of the arrangement could not be achieved?"

(iii) Do the parties to the arrangement have the power to disclose personal information for that purpose?

4. If the purpose cannot be achieved without sharing personal information, then each party to the arrangement will need to consider whether they have the power to disclose information for this purpose. This is particularly significant for public sector bodies or agencies whose powers and responsibilities are defined by statute or administrative law. If a public body acts *ultra vires* or outside its powers, then it may, at the same time, breach the lawfulness requirement of the first data protection principle. Section 115 of

the Crime and Disorder Act 1998 may provide the parties with the lawful power they need provided the requirements of that section are met. This provides that any person can lawfully disclose information, where necessary or expedient for the purposes of any provision of the (1998) Act, to a chief officer of police, a police authority, local authorities, Probation Service or health authority, even if they do not otherwise have this power. This power also covers disclosure to people acting on behalf of any of the above named bodies. The "purposes" of the Act referred to in Section 115 include a range of measures such as local crime audits, youth offending teams, anti-social behaviour orders, sex offender orders, and local child curfew schemes. It should also be noted that Section 17 of the Act places a statutory duty on every local authority to "exercise its various functions...with due regard to...the need to do all that it reasonably can to prevent...crime and disorder in its area".

(iv) How much personal information will need to be shared in order to achieve the objectives of the arrangement?

5.   Consideration must be given to the extent of any personal information disclosed. Some agencies may hold a lot of personal information on individuals but not all of this may be relevant to the purpose of the information sharing arrangement, so it may not be right to disclose it all. This is a matter for consideration by the agency holding the information.

(v) Should the consent of the individual be sought before disclosure is made?

6.   When disclosing personal information, many of the data protection issues surrounding disclosure can be avoided if the consent of the individual has been sought and obtained. This is particularly significant if the personal information to be shared identified victims or witnesses where consideration should be given to any effects of disclosure of their personal data on third parties.

(vi) What if the consent of the individual is not sought, or is sought but withheld?

7.   Consideration must be given to whether the personal information can be disclosed lawfully and fairly. In terms of *lawfulness*, an agency will need to consider whether personal information is held under a *duty of confidence*. If it is, then it may only be disclosed:

(a)   with the individual's consent; or

(b)   where there is an overriding public interest or justification for doing so.

It will not *always* be the case that the prevention and detection of crime or public safety constitutes an overriding public interest for the exchange of personal information.

8.   As regards fairness, even if the personal information held is not subject to a duty of confidence, the agency will still need to consider how the disclosure can be made fairly. In data protection terms, in order to obtain and process personal data fairly, the individual should be informed of any non-obvious uses (including disclosure) of their personal data, and be given the opportunity to consent to those uses. If consent is therefore not obtained, consideration will have to be given to how the disclosure can be made fairly. This might involve arguments of public interest, but these would have to be balanced against any potential resulting prejudice to the interests of the individual concerned.

(vii) How does the non-disclosure exemption apply?

9.   The Data Protection Acts 1984 and 1998 contain general "non-disclosure provisions",

but allow a number of specific exemptions. There is an exemption in both Acts which states that personal information may be disclosed for the purposes of the prevention or detection of crime, or the apprehension or prosecution of offenders, in cases where failure to disclose would be likely to prejudice those objectives. A party seeking to rely on this exemption needs to make a judgement as to whether, in the particular circumstances of an individual case, there would be a substantial chance that one or both of those objectives would be noticeably damaged if the personal information was withheld.

(viii) How do you ensure compliance with the other data protection principles?

10. Any information sharing arrangement should also address the following issues:

    * how will it be ensured that only the *minimum personal information necessary* is shared and held for the purpose(s) of the arrangement?

    * how will the *accuracy* of the personal information be maintained? One party to the arrangement may know that there has been a change in personal information which they have disclosed: how does that party ensure that all recipients of that personal information are kept informed of developments, so that they can keep their records up to date?

    * *for how long* will personal information be retained? It would be anomalous if the disclosing agency were to remove the personal information from its systems, but the other parties continued to hold it.

    * how will individuals be given *access* to personal information held about them? Under data protection legislation, individuals have a right of access to any information held about them. This right may be denied in certain limited circumstances, which include where access would prejudice the prevention or detection of crime. This could be significant, if, for example, a police force wished to disclose personal data to another party, but for operational reasons did not want the individual concerned to know the disclosure had been made. On the other hand, it is not sufficient to deny subject access merely because the information is held for crime prevention purposes. Mechanisms must therefore be in place to ensure that the wishes of the disclosing party are considered.

    * how will the personal data be *stored*? The more sensitive the personal data shared, the more security measures should be taken by each party receiving that personal data. This is not limited to physical security of the equipment on which it is held, but extends to technological security (for example, limited staff access, appropriate levels of staff access) and to staff security (staff with authorised access should be aware of its purpose and extent).

5

Individual Cases flow chart

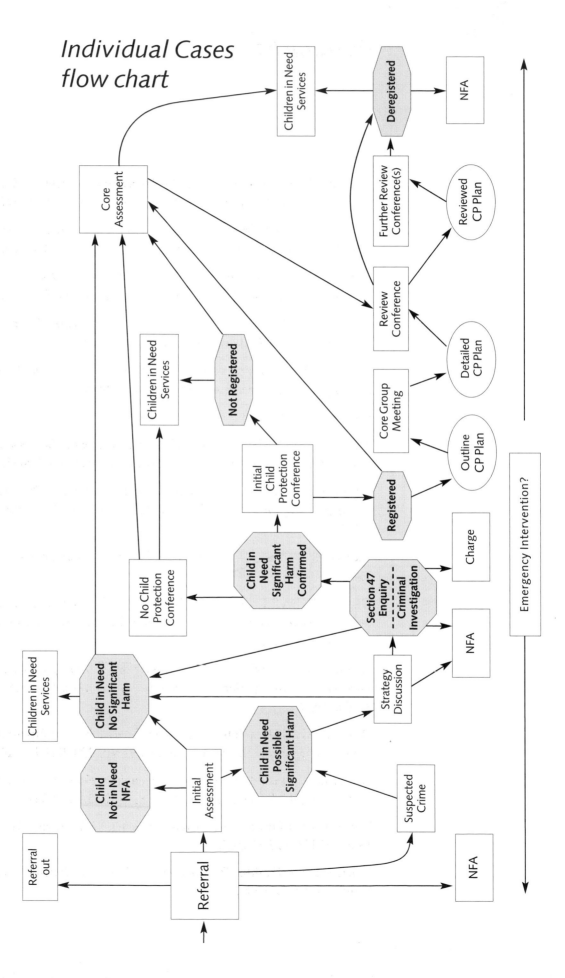

6

Reading list

The ABCD Consortium. *Abuse & Children who are Disabled: The ABCD Training and Resource Pack.* Bedfordshire: The ABCD Consortium, 1993. ISBN 0 902498 53 3.

Armstrong H. *A Safer Practice: A Child Protection Guide For GPs And The Primary Health Care Team.* Leicester: Community Education Development Centre, 1996.

Armstrong H. *What About The Child? Child Protection Training for Nurses.* Leicester: Community Education Development Centre, 1998. ISBN 0 947607 46 3.

Armstrong H, *Community Education Development Centre. Child Protection For Health Visitors: A Training Resource.* London: HMSO, 1994.

Calder M, Horwath J (eds.) *Working for Children on the Child Protection Register: an inter-agency guide.* Aldershot: Arena/Ashgate, 1999.

Children Act 1989. London: HMSO, 1989.

The Children's Society *Working With Sexually Abused Children: A Resource Pack for Professionals.* London: The Children's Society, 1998. ISBN 0 907324 398

Churches Child Protection Advisory Service. *Guidance to Churches Protecting children and appointing children's workers.* CCPAS (PO Box 133, Swanley, Kent, BR8 7N 0 9534355 0 4.

Cleaver H, Wattam C, Cawson P. *Assessing Risk in Child Protection.* London: NSPCC, 1998.

Cleaver H, Unell I, Aldgate J. *Children's Needs – Parenting Capacity: The impact of parental mental illness, problem alcohol and drug use, and domestic violence on children's development.* (In Press).

Connolly J, Shemmings D. *Undertaking Assessment of Children and Families – A Directory of Training Materials, Courses and Key Texts.* Norwich: University of East Anglia, 1999.

Davies G, Marshall E, Robertson N. *Child Abuse: Training Investigating Officers – Police Research Series Paper 94.* London: Home Office, 1999. ISBN 1 84082 148 5.

Department of Health. *Caring for Children Away From Home – Messages from Research.* Chichester: John Wiley & Sons Ltd, 1998. ISBN 0 -471 98475 2.

Department of Health. *An Introduction To The Children Act 1989.* London: HMSO, 1989. ISBN 0 11 321254 2

Department of Health. *The Children Act 1989 – an introductory guide for the NHS.* London: HMSO, 1989.

Department of Health. *The Children Act 1989 Guidance and Regulations Volume 1 – Court Orders.* London: HMSO, 1991. ISBN 0 11 321371 9.

Department of Health. *The Children Act 1989 Guidance and Regulations Volume 2 – Family Support, Day Care and Educational Provision for Young Children.* London: HMSO, 1991. ISBN 0 11 321372 7.

Department of Health. *The Children Act 1989 Guidance and Regulations Volume 3 – Family Placements.* HMSO, 1991. ISBN 0 11 321375 1.

Department of Health. *The Children Act 1989 Guidance and Regulations Volume 4 – Residential Care.* London: HMSO, 1991. ISBN 0 11 321430 8.

Department of Health. *The Children Act 1989 Guidance and Regulations Volume 5 – Independent Schools.* London: HMSO, 1991. ISBN 0 11 321373 5.

Department of Health. *The Children Act 1989 Guidance and Regulations Volume 6 – Children with Disabilities.* London: HMSO, 1991. ISBN 0 11 321452 9.

Department of Health. *The Children Act 1989 Guidance and Regulations Volume 7 – Guardians ad Litem and Other Court – Related Issues.* London: HMSO, 1991. ISBN 0 11 -321471 5.

Department of Health. *The Children Act 1989 Guidance and Regulations Volume 8 – Private Fostering and Miscellaneous.* London: HMSO, 1991. ISBN 0 11 321473 1.

Department of Health. *The Children Act 1989 Guidance and Regulations Volume 9 – Adoption Issues.* London: HMSO, 1991. ISBN 0 11 321474 X.

Department of Health. *The Children Act 1989 Guidance and Regulations Volume 10 – Index* London: HMSO, 1991. ISBN 0 11 321538 X.

Department of Health. *Child Protection – Clarification Of Arrangements Between The NHS And Other Agencies: Addendum To Working Together Under The Children Act 1989.* London: HMSO, 1995.

Department of Health. *Child Protection – Medical Responsibilities – Guidance to doctors working with Child Protection agencies: Addendum to Working Together under the Children Act 1989.* London: HMSO, 1996.

Department of Health. *Child Protection – Messages From Research.* London: HMSO, 1995. ISBN 0 11 321781 1.

Department of Health. *Framework for the Assessment of Children in Need and their Families.* London: The Stationery Office, 2000.

Department of Health. *Local Authority Circular LAC(93)17 Disclosure of Criminal Background of Those with Access to Children.* London: Department of Health, 1993.

Department of Health. *Local Authority Circular LAC(97)17: Guidance to the Children (Protection from Offenders) (Miscellaneous Amendments) Regulations SI 1997/2308.* London: Department of Health, 1997.

Department of Health. *Local Authority Circular LAC(99)33, Health Service Circular HSC 1999/237, DfEE Circular 18/99: The Quality Protects Programme : Transforming Children's Services 2000–01.* London: Department of Health, 1999.

Department of Health. *Social Services Inspectorate. The Challenge of Partnership in Child Protection: Practice Guide.* London: HMSO, 1995. ISBN 0 11 321825 7.

Department of Health. *Standing Nursing and Midwifery Advisory Committee. Child Protection: Guidance for Senior Nurses, Health Visitors and Midwives and their Managers.* London: The Stationery Office, 1997. ISBN 0 11 321999 7

Department of Health, The Welsh Office. *People Like Us – The Report of the Review of the Safeguards for Children Living Away From Home.* London: The Stationery Office, 1998. ISBN 0 11 322101 0

Falkov A, (ed). *Crossing Bridges – Parental Mental Illness and Its Implications for Children.* London: Department of Health, 1998. ISBN 1 900 600 49 8.

The Government's Response to the Children's Safeguards Review. London: The Stationery Office, 1998 (Cm. 4105). ISBN 0 10 141052-2.

Home Office. *Speaking Up for Justice. Report of the Interdepartmental Group on the Treatment of Vulnerable or Intimidated Witnesses in the Criminal Justice System.* London: The Stationery Office, 1998.

Home Office, Department of Health. *Memorandum of Good Practice on Video Recorded Interviews With Child Witnesses for Criminal Proceedings.* London: HMSO, 1992. ISBN 0 11 341040 9.

Jackson S, Kilroe S (eds). *Looking After Children: Good Parenting, Good Outcomes.* London: HMSO, 1995.

Jones D, Ramchandani P. *Child Sexual Abuse Informing Practice from Research.* Oxford: Radcliffe Medical Press, 1999. ISBN 85775 362 3.

Local Government Drugs Forum, *Standing Conference on Drug Abuse. Drug Using Parents – Policy Guidelines For Inter-Agency Working.* London: Local Government Association, 1997. ISBN 1 84049 010 1.

Morris K, Marsh P, Wiffin J. *Family Group Conferences – A Training Pack.* London: Family Rights Group, 1998.

NSPCC. *A Case For Balance – Demonstrating Good Practice When Children Are Witnesses.* London: NSPCC, 1997.

NSPCC. *Turning Points: A Resource Pack for Communicating With Children.* London: NSPCC, 1997.

NSPCC, Barnardo's, University of Bristol. *Making an Impact: Children and Domestic Violence: A Training and Resource Pack.* Bristol: University of Bristol, 1998.

NSPCC/ ChildLine. *The Young Witness Pack.* London: NSPCC/ChildLine, 1998. 42

NSPCC, University of Sheffield. *A Child's World.* Leicester: NSPCC, (in press).

Schonveld A. *Developing Your Child Protection Policy – Guidance For Schools.* Leicester: Community Education Development Centre, 1998. ISBN 0 94 760740 4.

University of East Anglia. *Learning How to Make Children Safer: an analysis for the Welsh Office of serious child abuse cases in Wales.* Welsh Office, 1999.